How to use **ICT**
to support children with
**special educational
needs**

**Anne Sparrowhawk
and
Ysanne Heald**

Acknowledgements

Over the last 12 years we have been excited to see the opportunities created by the use of ICT in a wide variety of educational contexts. Writing this book has provided us with a great opportunity to focus on how ICT supports learners with special needs and the adults who work with them. We have experienced the passion of many dedicated professionals who strive to find tools and resources which enable those with special needs to experience an inclusive education.

We are particularly appreciative of the help and time given to us by Nicola Davies, who shared many experiences of working with nursery and early years children; Terry Holmes, who supplied the information on ADHD; Angela Jones, who advised on the use of interactive whiteboards; Patsy Deller, a headteacher who gave real examples of how inclusivity works in her school and how those with diverse specific needs are catered for; Sue Smith, who offered insight as an ICT co-ordinator; Ed Clark, who informed us about the role of the TA's play with children with physical difficulties; Chris Stevens, who shared his experience of managing the CAP project; and Tina Detheridge, whose advice on communicating using symbols proved invaluable. Our grateful thanks also go to the many software publishers, manufacturers and distributors who were willing to share their experiences with us.

We believe we have, at this time, a great opportunity to continue the development of ICT to support children with SEN, their teachers, parents and carers. And it seems the whole community is eager to work together to provide the environment and resources to ensure every child matters. So many thanks to all who have been involved in working with us, including Debbie Pullinger for her effective editing and LDA for publishing the work.

How to use ICT to support children with special educational needs

MT10166

ISBN-13: 978 1 88503 420 4

© Ysanne Heald and Anne Sparrowhawk

Cover illustration: © Rebecca Barnes

Inside illustration: © Rebecca Barnes

All rights reserved

First published 2007

Reprinted 2008

Printed in the UK for LDA

Abbeygate House, East Road, Cambridge, CB1 1DB, UK

Contents

Contents

Introduction

Information and communication technology (ICT) is fundamentally a tool. It helps us write, store and retrieve information in many different formats; it helps us organise ideas and share them with other people, either in the same room or far away. This book focuses on ways in which this tool can best be used to serve the learning needs of children, and of those with special educational needs (SEN) in particular. It looks at how we can ensure that the ICT used in schools is accessible to all pupils, and at what specific ICT solutions will engage those with SEN and facilitate their learning.

Who will benefit from this book?

This book does not set out to prove that ICT is some sort of universal solution that will meet all the learning needs of children with SEN. Rather, we suggest some classroom approaches and some ways of using ICT that can support the learning needs of these children and allow them to demonstrate their skills successfully. Many of the ideas in this book have been drawn from teachers who work with children with SEN every day in mainstream classrooms. The book will therefore be of interest to class teachers, SENCos and teaching assistants (TAs) in primary schools.

In beginning to think about ICT and SEN, the question arises: from which direction should we approach the subject – starting from the ICT or starting with the child? Whilst our underpinning philosophy is one of beginning with the child, we know also that what is needed is some kind of framework for assessing and selecting from the vast array of resources available. So in this book we have approached, as it were, from both sides. In Chapter 2, we provide an overview of the types of hardware and software and other ICT solutions that may be useful in a variety of situations. Then in Chapter 3 we look at the use of interactive whiteboards (IWBs) – both at the issues that may arise for children with SEN and the potential for supporting them. We go on in Chapter 4 to take some broad categories of educational need and look at what kind of ICT resources may be appropriate in each. In Chapter 5 we look at how ICT can assist SENCos in their role, including their work with parents. Chapter 6 supplements all the information in earlier chapters, with guidance on self-evaluation and details of resources.

We begin in Chapter 1 by considering the opportunities and challenges of inclusion in relation to the use of ICT, looking specifically at recent government initiatives that have stressed the need for ICT to contribute effectively to children's learning in a wide variety of contexts and situations.

Chapter 1
ICT and SEN

Only a few years ago, teaching children with special needs was considered a job for specially trained 'experts', but now it is the expectation that every teacher has the skills and ability to cater for all children, whatever their specific needs. Now that only those with severe SEN are catered for in special schools, headteachers in mainstream schools are responsible for providing a fully inclusive education and a learning environment which caters for the needs of the majority of children within the community. Indeed, inclusion is one of the four statutory general requirements of the National Curriculum, which says that schools must:

- ❍ set suitable learning challenges;
- ❍ respond to pupils' diverse learning needs;
- ❍ overcome potential barriers to learning and assessment for individuals and groups of pupils.

The government strategy challenges teachers to personalise learning for all children, to make education more innovative and responsive to the diverse needs of individual children and to raise their level of achievement.

www.audit-commission.gov.uk/reports

An Audit Commission report, *Special Educational Needs: a mainstream issue* (2002), suggested that one in five children is considered to have SEN. The category of special educational needs includes children with physical difficulties (including visual or auditory impairments) and those with learning difficulties that do not stem from any physical impairment. It also includes those children whose reading, writing and numeracy skills develop slowly. (Gifted and talented children are also recognised as having individual learning needs but these are not within the scope of this book.) Schools, therefore, need to know how to provide for a very wide range of different special needs amongst a diverse population that might include those with dyslexia, physical disabilities, speech and language disorders, visual impairment, hearing loss, difficulties in communication, and emotional and behavioural difficulties, to name but a few. The same research also reported that many staff feel ill-equipped to meet the wide range of pupils' needs in today's classrooms. School development plans will undoubtedly be addressing this challenge.

The impact of ICT

ICT is no longer just another teaching tool or another subject on the curriculum.

Computers have now been used in schools for over twenty years. For a long time there has been an expectation that ICT will change the way we teach and the way children learn, but only relatively recently has there been a sense of that change really beginning to take place. ICT is no longer just another teaching tool or another subject on the curriculum, but something that is starting to transform the whole education system. This transformation is being made possible for a number of reasons:

- Most schools now have an infrastructure that offers a reliable network of desktop and laptop computers, giving both teachers and pupils easy access to the technology.
- Wireless networks are providing access throughout school buildings and grounds, so rather than the learners having to move to the location of the technology, the technology can be brought to the learner – when and where they need it.
- Accessibility devices mean that children of almost all physical abilities can now benefit from computers.
- Broadband connectivity gives schools a fast and effective means of communication and the opportunity to have a wide range of multimedia content delivered online. For children with special needs, the opportunity to watch videos or listen to audio clips can be especially beneficial.
- Interactive whiteboards (IWBs) and digital projectors allow teachers to integrate ICT into their lessons and to cater for a wide range of abilities in their classes.
- There is now a wealth of high quality educational software offering content for use within the curriculum as well as tools that enable the learner to access the curriculum or to be creative in their delivery of work. Many programs have features to support a wide range of learners, and some are designed specifically to support children with special needs.

And often, it is in a special-needs context that new ideas are tried out.

Unquestionably one of the most important influences on the success of ICT in schools is the confidence of teachers and their enthusiasm to make it work. And often, it is in a special-needs context that new ideas are tried out and that teachers work together to understand the benefits and find solutions. More parents, too, may be in a position to offer support at home and have ICT resources that provide some continuity between home and school.

Food for thought
- There is more than one school computer for every eight primary children.
- 99 per cent of primary schools are connected to the Internet and 78 per cent have broadband connection.
- One in four primary school lessons now uses technology.

Statistics taken from *Harnessing Technology* (2005)

ICT offers a vast range of resources for teachers and learners. Used effectively, these resources can empower and motivate all learners and ease the administrative load for all teachers. Children with SEN can benefit from ICT in many of the ways that all children benefit; there are also additional ways in which these children may be helped by the use of ICT.

Ways ICT can help

www.teachernet.gov.uk/ wholeschool/sen/senstrategy

The use of ICT to help improve education for children with SEN and disabilities is strongly encouraged by government strategy. *Removing Barriers to Achievement* (2004) describes a role for ICT in all four of its key areas: Early intervention, Removing barriers to learning, Raising expectations and achievement, and Delivering improvements in partnership. The list below

indicates some of the ways in which ICT can bring specific benefits to children with SEN within all of those areas.

Increasing motivation

Most children are motivated by technology. It empowers them, gives them confidence and enables them to communicate and learn effectively. It can help some children overcome communication difficulties, so that they can be included in lessons and can access a wider curriculum.

Improving access

ICT can enable children with a variety of physical disabilities to achieve the same learning outcomes as the rest of the class. A child who is struggling with handwriting might be given a keyboard to produce their work; another the opportunity to respond to visual clues to demonstrate understanding, rather than having to write responses down; another might read the screen more easily when the colour and contrast of the text are changed.

Removing Barriers to Achievement (2004) also envisages that the development of virtual communities will make it easier to innovate and collaborate, to share resources, to exchange ideas and work with others to solve problems and generally to communicate more effectively.

Raising expectations and achievement

ICT can help children with learning difficulties achieve higher standards. For example, a child who is a reluctant reader will benefit from the auditory and visual impact of multimedia presentations on deepening their understanding and ensuring progression in teaching and learning.

Facilitating differentiation

Raising expectations and achievement focuses attention on personalised learning for children with SEN. With much educational software, teachers can tailor the content to meet the precise requirements of children with special needs; for example, changing text to speech, altering colours on the screen, increasing the size of text and specifying levels of differentiation in activities. For some children, access to appropriate ICT solutions may be the only way for them to communicate with their peers and realise their full potential.

Providing alternatives

ICT offers alternative models for engaging pupils in learning, and sometimes trial and error will reveal what works best with individual children. For example, some children are naturally independent learners, whilst others are stimulated by working with peers on collaborative projects – a child who may not be capable of working on a large project alone may work well as a key member of a team – offering ideas, producing a video or publishing a website.

Engaging with the real world

Technology is now a huge part of life, so by helping children to become confident and competent with ICT, we are equipping them with the skills they will need now and in the future. Young children should therefore be introduced to relevant technology in role-play situations such as 'going to the supermarket', where they use bar codes, calculators and tills, or 'a visit to hospital', where they book appointments using computers or interpret images on screen. Older children might be encouraged to appreciate real-life scenarios and be given problem-solving tasks which build their confidence in handling everyday situations.

Facilitating assessment

There are many software packages that enable the teacher to keep track of what children have achieved. They usually provide an overview of what has been covered as well as a detailed summary of specific skills learned. These can be helpful in revealing gaps in a child's understanding. Some of these packages offer a target-setting option whilst others leave the target-setting to the teacher. But as well as deciding what will best suit your needs, you will have to consider what will help and motivate your children most effectively.

Of course, ICT offers the possibility of easier assessment and information gathering, but the onus is on the school to make good use of the information they collect and to analyse how children with SEN are progressing.

Supporting administration

All teachers spend a considerable amount of time dealing with the administrative burden that now goes with the job. This is usually even more demanding for teachers dealing with SEN children, especially when they have statements and a wider team of support workers with whom communication is required. The SENCo has responsibilities that are particularly time consuming. Thankfully, technology can help to reduce this load. It can offer an effective means of communication between the school and parents and children; it can provide a structured model for assessment and target-setting; and it can facilitate demonstrating evidence of progress. *Removing Barriers to Achievement* (2004) acknowledges the pressing need to reduce bureaucracy, enabling staff to spend their time with pupils rather than on paperwork – which will help in working towards the objective of early intervention. Thus, schools and early years settings are being encouraged to focus on the essentials and make better use of ICT for recording and for reducing administration.

Supporting home and community links

ICT can promote practice that reaches beyond the school into homes and the community, increasing access and inclusiveness. For a child with a long-term illness, for example, online learning resources could be made available via the Internet so the child can continue with their learning from home or hospital. Again, this is endorsed by *Removing Barriers to Learning*, which suggests that technology used effectively will facilitate personalised learning as well as active communication and collaboration between parents, children and schools.

As a rule, general good practice in the use of ICT will benefit those with learning difficulties.

A note on access

Ensuring that children with special needs can access ICT resources is not only an important consideration, but also a legal requirement. It is about making sure that ICT is used inclusively, taking full account of the ways in which ICT can be made accessible to all. As a rule, following general good practice in the use of ICT will benefit those with learning difficulties, and many of the ideas in this book are simply about good general practice. In addition, there will be particular measures that will benefit children with SEN, such as hardware that supports children with visual, physical or auditory impairment and computer programs that specifically cater for the needs of children with learning difficulties.

ICT and government strategy

> We will encourage through our ICT in Schools and E-learning strategies the wider use of ICT to improve access to education for children with SEN and disabilities
>
> *Removing Barriers to Achievement* (2004)

Now that nearly all schools are connected to the Internet, an increasing number via broadband, and most families have access to a computer and the Internet in their own home or through local community facilities, the potential for ICT to support learning has changed. This has been reflected in a number of recent government strategy documents, including the SEN strategy, *Removing Barriers to Achievement*. The report encourages schools and early years settings to make better and wider use of ICT in support of all the areas listed above.

The changing role of technology in education is tackled head-on in *Harnessing Technology: transforming learning and children's services* (2005). This document acknowledges that although the use of ICT in education has come a long way, development has been somewhat 'haphazard'. It seeks to bring about a more strategic approach to its future development and suggests how digital and interactive technologies can be used to achieve a more personalised approach within all areas of education and children's services. It sets out four main objectives, which can be summarised as follows:

- ◗ to transform teaching, learning and child development, enabling children and learners of all ages to meet their highest expectations;

- ◗ to connect with hard-to-reach groups in new ways;

- ◗ to open up education to partnerships with other organisations;

- ◗ to move to a new level of efficiency and effectiveness in delivery.

To achieve these objectives, it proposes a strategy that has the following priorities:
- an integrated online information service for all citizens;
- integrated online personal support for children and learners;
- a collaborative approach to personalised learning activities;
- a good quality training and support package for practitioners;
- a leadership and development package for organisational capability in ICT;
- a common digital infrastructure to support transformation and reform.

Harnessing Technology (2005)

Further change in the education system is being wrought by The Children Act 2004, and the resulting initiative *Every Child Matters*. The government's aim is for every pupil, whatever their background or their circumstances, to have the support they need to:

● be healthy;

● stay safe;

● enjoy and achieve;

● make a positive contribution;

● achieve economic well-being.

One way of achieving this will be to establish integrated working within children's services to improve outcomes for children. This major development requires change in culture and practice across the workforce of all those teaching and supporting children. Education, health and social service workers, parents and carers all have their own expertise and their particular knowledge and understanding of every child for whom they are responsible. This new structure is intended to offer a better environment for these people to share information effectively and for this to be used to help each child to achieve the five aims. Again, ICT has an important role to play, and will provide support for schools and teachers in the following forms:

● **Online training materials and information** – which will be available at a national and local level. Local websites may be effective in providing local information for parents, teachers and community workers.

● **The Information Sharing Index** – a national database of practitioners delivering services to children, enabling practitioners to contact one another quickly and easily in order to share information about individual children. This is due to be implemented by the end of 2008.

● **Local online communities** – these will facilitate effective communication and collaboration between teams of professionals.

So, as a result of government directives, ICT is set to play an ever-increasing part in the education system. Setting the framework for learning, however, is not just a case of ticking off achievements for the government.

Assessing ICT for SEN in your school

Research by Becta in 2004 showed that teachers can maximise the impact of ICT in inclusive classrooms by:

● understanding the potential of ICT to support learners with special needs;

● training classroom assistants in how software and devices can be used;

● tailoring and adapting tasks to suit individual students' abilities and skills.

For a general audit of ICT provision throughout the school, Becta provides a valuable self-review framework (see Chapter 6). You may also find it helpful to look more specifically at ICT in relation to special needs. A self-audit offers a valuable tool with which to map provision requirements. It should focus

ICT is set to play an ever-increasing part in the education system.

attention on the whole-school issues of teaching and learning as well as on individual needs. A suggested framework for carrying out such an audit is provided on pages 12–13. The audit will have an impact on the whole school, and it is important that the SENCo and headteacher work in partnership to ensure that both the strategy and ways to implement it are firmly in place.

As a result of the self-audit, your school will be able to:

- ❍ identify individual needs;
- ❍ understand the value of resources;
- ❍ match provision to needs and identify gaps;
- ❍ cost provision requirements accurately;
- ❍ make proposals for resource or budget requirements for SEN within the school and cater for specific needs;
- ❍ assess the effectiveness of resources linked to outcomes;
- ❍ inform staff, parents, governors, the local authority (LA) and other agencies about how resources are being used to meet needs;
- ❍ provide information that is transferred with children to new classes or schools.

consider also possible ways to make the most of available funding

Provision needs can be mapped in different ways. They could, for example, be mapped against year group or key stage, or according to the SEN Code of Practice. If mapped against the Code of Practice, they could be allocated by the School Action wave of support and the School Action Plus wave. Providing technology solutions for children with special needs can be expensive and relies on adequate funding for SEN. Consider possible ways to make the most of funding available, for example:

- ❍ Are there some resources that could be shared with another school?
- ❍ Can you buy resources at the same time as another school or schools so as to benefit from a quantity discount?
- ❍ If you have purchased resources for children who have left the school, are there other local schools that would benefit from being loaned the equipment?
- ❍ Children with statements are usually given the resources they need, but would others benefit from the investment in technology? For example, teachers have observed that many reluctant writers develop greater confidence and self-esteem when provided with a laptop.

Assessing ICT and SEN checklist

The school	Comments
Working in multidisciplinary teams presents new challenges in communication. Are you guided by models of good practice both from within your LA and from other areas?	
Have you considered and built an effective communication strategy, which defines: • information to be recorded; • the format and audience for different types of information; • how this information supports teaching and learning?	
Is adequate attention given to the role of ICT for children with SEN, and to the skills needed by staff supporting those children?	
Is there an ICT link governor and an SEN link governor on the school's governing body? If so, are these members of the governing body actively involved in evaluating and monitoring the role of ICT in supporting children with SEN?	
Resources	
Is there adequate funding allocated to ICT for children with SEN, especially for those who do not have statements?	
Has the school identified what resources and expertise are available locally to support children?	
Is the school actively participating in any virtual networks? These can offer valuable communication, providing advice, reaching 'experts' and solving problems.	
Are there any expensive resources that could be either shared with another school or purchased at the same time as another school makes purchases, to benefit from a bulk order discount?	

Assessing ICT and SEN checklist

Staff	Comments
Are all staff, teachers and TAs confident in their own use of ICT? Do they understand: • the potential of ICT to support learners and what benefits it can bring to the learning environment; • how to select suitable resources to support learning; • how to manage learning using those resources?	
Is there an agreed specification of the core skills required by all staff and the advanced skills required by particular staff?	
Is there sufficient investment in training for all staff, whether through learning from other teachers, visiting other schools or attending formal training courses?	
Are all staff aware of security and confidentiality issues when information is handled through ICT?	
When SEN children enter the school, is there a check on what ICT resources have supported and motivated them previously?	
Links with home and community	
Do you know which parents have access to a computer and the Internet at home?	
For those who don't, what does the school offer to facilitate access?	
Does your school website support children learning at home? Can children access the work they have done at school while at home, either to share it with their parents or to continue the work?	
When setting up extended school provision, have you considered the role of ICT, considering: • how it can be used for the benefit of the children; • how it can assist your communication with the local community?	

Chapter 2
Choosing hardware and software

Making the best use of ICT depends on having both the hardware and the software that matches your children's needs. In this chapter, we shall look at the following:

- ◗ **Hardware** – how you can ensure the computers in your school meet the needs of all the children you teach. This might mean adding special devices so that a child can access the computer and use it more effectively, or purchasing special equipment to support the needs of individual children.

- ◗ **Software** – how to choose the programs that will best support the children you teach. These could include software to support subjects and topics that you are teaching and provide content tailored to the needs and abilities of children with special needs – thus supporting inclusion and differentiation. Other software might facilitate access to learning resources, for example packages that allow children to dictate information to the computer, or to use symbols as a means of written communication.

- ◗ **Accessibility features** – how you can configure the access to the school's computer network to support children who find the standard interface difficult. There are ways of saving settings for individual children so that the right settings automatically become available when a particular child logs on to the computer.

Assessing needs

When deciding what hardware and software to choose for a child with disabilities or SEN, it is important to look at the child and their needs, and also at the context – the environment, the tools and the learning tasks. Clearly this is not a one-off undertaking, but an ongoing monitoring of the child's needs according to their changing requirements, the classroom environment and resources, and the learning tasks in hand. The checklist opposite may serve as a useful reminder of the factors that you will need to consider.

Assessing ICT requirements for a child with SEN

Context	The issues	School situation
The child	Are there barriers to using hardware? Have you watched the child using a computer and do you know where their difficulties lie? Is the child able to use the standard interfaces (mouse, keyboard, etc.)? Can they see the screen adequately? Can they hear the audio output clearly?	
	Are there barriers to using software? Is the child able to use the software that other class members use, or will they need materials that are differently paced and presented?	
	What are the child's preferred learning styles? Most software is predominantly visual; does the child need to engage kinaesthetically or in other ways?	
	Does the child need help to access resources? Could ICT offer help with communication or presentation of information through, for example, different screen formats or text-to-speech facilities?	
The learning task	What curriculum areas need to be covered? Are there any specific curriculum resources that might be helpful?	
	Which parts of the learning may be problematic? Is it in accessing the material or in producing their response that the child needs most help?	
	Does the child need help with understanding the content? Might software offer a means of simplifying information or concepts to make them more accessible to the child? How will the child access the stimulus materials?	
	What output is required? What do you want the child to produce in response? Can ICT assist?	

Assessing ICT requirements for a child with SEN

Context	The issues	School situation
The tools	What hardware is needed? What hardware solution is available within school?	
	What software is available? Is there additional software that might help the child as well as the resources that the other children use?	
	What teaching and learning strategies need to be supported by ICT resources? Will the child need to work on their own after the stimulus part of the lesson?	
The environment	Where will ICT be used? Will the child be able to use the ICT in the same location as other children? Will they need to have different access?	
	What support is available? Will the child need help from an adult to access the activity, or could another child provide the necessary support?	
	How will you assess achievement? How will you assess what the child has achieved? Will ICT contribute to assessment? Will the achievements be different from those of the other children in the class?	

© *How to use ICT to support children with special educational needs* LDA

Hardware

There are a great many hardware products for special needs on the market, and far too many for all to be included here. The products we have described below are those most likely to be relevant for SEN children in mainstream education, and they will give you an idea of the kind of things that are available. However, this is only a selection, and it is well worth browsing the catalogues of specialist suppliers for products that may be just what you need for a particular child or for your particular situation. (See Chapter 6 for details.)

The list includes a number of special devices that facilitate computer access and thus enable children with particular needs or disabilities to become more independent in a mainstream classroom and to benefit from learning opportunities alongside their peers. We have also included items that might be considered 'standard kit', which have nevertheless proved to have a particular relevance to children with SEN.

Computer peripherals
Wireless keyboard and mouse
For children who find it difficult to get physically close to a computer desk, a wireless keyboard and mouse can be a good solution.

Scanner
Useful for capturing images, graphics and drawings, a scanner allows you to include the child's work in a class presentation, or provides a starting point for their writing.

Good quality printer
Children take great pride in the finished product, and this requires a good quality printer – probably one that prints in colour. The immediacy of having a piece of finished work to take home can be very positive for children with SEN.

Adjustable computer trolley
With an adjustable computer trolley, all children, including those in wheelchairs or using frames, can use the computer at the right height.

Switches
A switch acts as an alternative input mechanism for the computer or other electronic device. It can be operated by a hand, a head or any other part of the body which the child is able to control. It is possible to attach switches to battery-powered toys, mains-powered equipment and simple speech output devices in order to help younger or less able children grasp the 'cause and effect' concept.

It may take some children time to develop the skills needed to use a switch successfully. A switch may need to be pressed several times for even the simplest of operations to be carried out, requiring both physical and cognitive effort from the child.

There is some mainstream software which can be used with switches, but specialised software is usually required. In order for the computer to interpret commands from the switch, an interface device is needed. Scanning is a common selection method for this interpretation. This requires the child to select from items that are presented to them (i.e. pictures, symbols, words) by making contact with the switch.

There are many different types of switches available. The most common are those that are activated by a touch or press from a body part. These are available in many different shapes, colours and sizes. The amount of force or pressure required to operate the switch also varies. Most switches today are sensitive across their whole surface. Below are some examples of touch-activated switches. There are a number of other types of switch available for children with severe physical impairment. The ACE Centre is a good source of advice on these (see Chapter 6); suppliers include Crick and Inclusive Technology.

www.ace-centre.org.uk

A large switch which is responsive across the whole surface

Some switches are activated by being pushed in a number of directions by a body movement, returning to the 'neutral' position once released. This type of switch is useful for children who have random or uncontrollable movements. These switches include 'wobble' and 'leaf' switches. They can be operated using the head and usually require mounting.

Wobble switch

Crick USB switch box

The Crick switch box provides reliable switch access via a standard USB port. It is 'plug and play' and will work with Clicker and nearly all switch-accessible software. The box comes with Cricksoft's USB Keys software, which enables you to set up switch presses to convert into key presses or mouse clicks.

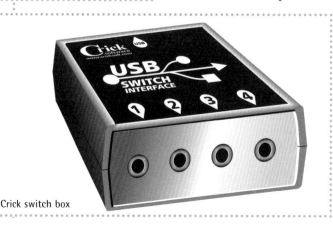

Crick switch box

www.cricksoft.com

BIGmack

The BIGmack stores a voice message of up to 20 seconds' duration, which can then be replayed with a single press of the switch. Recording is very quick and easy, so the message can be changed as required. This device is useful for putting switch activity into a social and communication context, and it is especially useful with children who are more interested in people than things. There are all sorts of possibilities for using the BIGmack: a child can use it to take messages to another class, to answer their name, and to join in with a song or story with a repeated phrase, or to give an instruction to someone in a group.

BIGmack

Battery switch adaptor

This allows you to adapt a battery-powered toy so that it can be turned on and off easily by means of a large switch. Using the switch to operate the toy can reinforce the child's concept of cause and effect.

Computer input devices

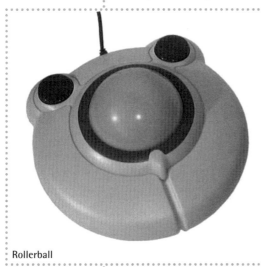

Rollerball

Rollerball

Some children who find it difficult to use a mouse find it easier to use a rollerball because it is stationary. You simply roll the ball to move the cursor. Rollerballs are available in a variety of shapes and sizes, and some have additional features to slow down the movements that cause interaction. For children who have difficulty with finer movements, a rollerball with a switch connection is also available.

Joystick

Joysticks developed for special needs are easier to use than a mouse. They dampen down the random motion and thus ensure that the movement is less erratic. They can be found on most electric wheelchairs and often operate computer games. The Inclusive EasiTrax joystick combines the strengths of a rollerball and a joystick. It is light and easy to use, requiring minimal hand movements to operate.

Touch pads

Touch pads are useful for children who lack gross hand movement but have fine finger control. The child interacts with the computer using either a finger or a special pen.

Touch screen

Touch screens are valuable for children with co-ordination problems and for those who cannot understand the relationship between the mouse or keyboard and the movement on screen. Most educational software works with touch screens once the software drivers which come with your screen are installed on your computer. Children point directly at the screen to move objects around, choose options or follow a sequence as it develops on screen. There are different types of touch screen:

- ● interactive whiteboards (effectively large touch screens);
- ● touch-screen monitors;
- ● touch-screen attachments which are placed over monitors.

Touch-screen monitors are generally large and heavy, which may be considered an advantage because it means the screen won't be pushed away when the child touches it. However, they do take up more desk space. Different touch screens work in different ways: with some you have to use a special pen or a stylus, but others can be activated with a finger. Screens also vary in their clarity of image and their durability. It is therefore important to consider your children's needs and to look at the features of different models before purchasing a touch screen.

Special computers
Laptop word processor

www.alphasmart.co.uk

Simple, easy-to-use laptops, such as Alphasmart Neo, come with a word-processing program designed specifically for educational purposes, and can be very useful for encouraging children to write. Predictive text allows children to focus on whole words rather than having to wrestle with each letter of every word, enabling them to transfer their thoughts to writing more easily. The LCD screen displays text at a readable size, and the whole machine is light yet robust. It comes with software installed and ready to use, and saving and printing are easy. The text may also be exported to a standard PC, where the child can then be encouraged to focus on the formatting of the text.

Laptop word processor

Spellchecker

Hand-held spellcheckers can be an enormous help to children who are poor spellers. 'Phonetic spellcheckers', such as those in the Franklin range, are best because they pick up errors based on likely letter–sound correspondence. They check the spelling of over 90,000 words and offer definitions and a thesaurus. Many also include word games which can help children improve their spelling.

Other equipment
Digital camera

Digital cameras are a particularly effective way to enhance project work and support the development of literacy skills. Captured moments from a school trip, visual reminders of a Lego model made last week and photos of significant people in a child's life can all stimulate writing and talking.

Digital video camera

Used in drama, sign-language classes, speech lessons and so on, a digital video camera can capture important moments and allow them to be discussed and reviewed later, motivating the children and keeping them engaged.

Headphones with boom microphone

Good quality headphones with a speech-recognition microphone are a valuable resource for many learners in busy, noisy classrooms. The headphones allow the child to hear the model speech from a computer clearly and the microphone allows them to input their own speech.

Mobile phone

Mobile phones are quite popular in the deaf / hard-of-hearing community because of the text message facility. The fact that texting is visual means that deaf and hard-of-hearing users can participate on an equal footing with hearing peers in this aspect of youth culture. Whilst you might not want all the children in your class to have their own mobile phone, this might be a valuable group activity to engage children who have hearing impairment.

PDA

A personal digital assistant (PDA) is a mini-computer that usually has a text editor, calendar, email program and web browser as well as other software. PDAs can be useful for children who need support in organising themselves.

Videophone and videoconferencing

These offer two-way, real-time audio and visual communication at a distance. Both technologies allow for communication with deaf or hearing people in sign language, either directly or through an interpreter.

Portable CCTV magnifiers

Portable CCTV magnifiers can be used for viewing documents close-to or images or activities at a distance. They can be useful for visually impaired learners who require magnification for close or distance work, or both. The live images appear on the screen at the selected magnification and resolution. Some systems have their own screens; others, such as Magnilink, connect easily to a computer or laptop.

Software

Working on a computer using well-designed software can have huge benefits for children with SEN:

- The interactivity promotes active learning and encourages the child to use their initiative to experiment, to solve problems and to make mistakes.
- Many programs lend themselves to collaborative learning, thus encouraging children with SEN to work with their peers.

● The child is encouraged to develop the ability to work independently, which in turn helps to develop confidence.

● It is a safe environment where children usually feel happy to try things out. Software is very patient and tolerant of mistakes. The concern about getting answers wrong in front of others is removed, so children have the opportunity to experience failure and to overcome it.

There are many types of educational software available, and sometimes you may be able to take software that you are using with the rest of the class and adapt it for use with children with SEN. In other situations it may be more appropriate to have software designed to meet particular educational needs. There are a huge number of educational software resources which claim to address the needs of children with learning difficulties, and it can be quite a challenge to sift through and select what is most appropriate for your children and your teaching context. Well-designed software that will support children with SEN is likely to:

● have a clear learning objective;

● be stimulating and fun;

● have colourful, clear graphics and interesting sounds;

● offer immediate feedback, rewarding success and offering help with errors; it is also valuable to have some summative feedback on completion of tasks;

● be patient, allowing the child to keep having another try;

● offer structured learning in small steps, ideally offering the facility to customise the size of the steps.

Exercises or activities are usually graded by difficulty; if this is the case, then it is helpful if the sequence of activities can be entered at a point appropriate to the learner. Some programs offer an initial assessment of ability and then provide a programme of activities based on the results.

It is particularly worth looking at how the software deals with errors. Does it model the correct answer? Does it repeat the task? Does it organise subsequent tasks accordingly? Does it provide relevant instruction?

In selecting software, it is important to consider the individual needs of the child, the specific setting and the objectives you hope to achieve. The checklist opposite offers some criteria that may help you with evaluation and selection.

Choosing software for children with SEN

Educational value and content	
What goals and objectives will this software help the children achieve?	
How does the program fit the curriculum or an individual education plan?	
Does it complement other learning activities that are going on in the classroom?	
Are there options that allow the teacher to tailor the program for different learners (e.g. changing level of difficulty, customisation of menus, varying rate of delivery, user preferences)?	
If there are questions on the screen, can you control how many are presented at once?	
Does it offer the right amount of text or information – or is there too much?	
Is the level of the language appropriate – or is it too difficult?	
Is the presentation of information appropriate for the children who will use it?	
Is there speech support that the children can control?	

Choosing software for children with SEN

Design and navigation	
Is the screen design simple, clear and uncluttered?	
Will it be easy for children with special needs to navigate around the program?	
Is the navigation consistent? (e.g. are the buttons in the same place on every screen?)	
Are there options that allow the teacher to tailor the appearance of the program for individual learners? (e.g. can you adjust size and style of text, colour of the background?)	
Ease of use and control	
How easy will it be for children to work independently with the software (if required), following initial teacher guidance?	
Are there settings that prevent children clicking out of the program, if that would aid their independence?	
Can the software be used with alternative input devices (e.g. switches) for children who need them?	
For programs where content can be created by the user, how easy is it to input information?	
Is there a management system that allows the teacher to track children's usage and progress? Is it easy to use? Is the information it provides useful?	
Is the software suitable for running on your computer? (Have you checked that the specification of your computer matches or exceeds the minimum specification required by the software?)	

There is a vast range of educational software to choose from. The following list provides only a very few examples of tried-and-tested products; see Chapter 6 for a list of software publishers, including some specialising in products for special needs.

Content-rich software
Skill Builders Vol. 2 – Matching Skills (Sherston)

Many programs for young children are rich in visual stimuli and offer too many distractions to make them suitable for children with SEN. The Skill Builder series offers a very clear interface which helps the child to focus on the task. This particular title teaches children to match by size, shape and colour, and to consider the criteria by which things are matched. The program also provides opportunities for vocabulary extension through discussion in pairs or small groups.

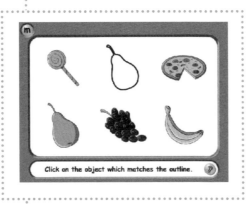

www.sherston.co.uk

ClozePro (Crick)

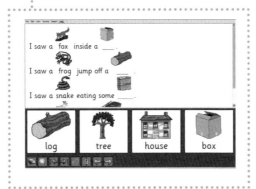

www.cricksoft.com

ClozePro provides a variety of cloze activities in which children click on letters, words or phrases in the grid to fill the highlighted gaps in the text. The program offers the teacher structured reports on an individual child's progress, including information on the prompts used and the attempts made. ClozePro has a wide range of accessibility options for children who cannot use a mouse, and may also be used to create paper-based cloze activities.

Software for customising resources
SwitchIt! Jigsaw Maker 2 (Inclusive Technology)

This program allows you to make your own photos or pictures into on-screen jigsaw puzzles with two, four or nine pieces. A puzzle can then be completed in any of four different ways which provide a progression in skills – from pressing a switch to see the picture built through to dragging pieces into the correct places. The program can be used with a standard mouse, with one or two switches, with a touch screen or with an IWB.

www.inclusive.co.uk

Clicker 5 (Crick)

Clicker 5 is a powerful and easy-to-use writing support and multimedia tool. Children can use the program to create a piece of work using whole words, phrases or pictures; they can also include animation and video and record their own speech. The program has a speech-support facility that means children can choose to hear any word or sentence spoken, simply by clicking on it. Clicker comes with its own picture library but other images can be used as well. The program allows the teacher to define the vocabulary that will be made available to the child, and can be used with a number of access devices, such as switches, for those who cannot operate a mouse.

www.cricksoft.com

Rebus symbols

Science symbols

Makaton signs and symbols

www.widgit.com
www.makaton.org

Alternative writing methods
Widgit

Widgit specialise in educational software for improving communication and literacy. In particular they produce a number of symbol-writing programs for various symbol systems that can be used to facilitate communication for all children. Those most commonly used in the UK are Widgit Rebus Symbols, Pictorial Communication Symbols (PCS) and the Makaton signs and symbols. The Makaton set of symbols for use with the software are purchased separately from the Makaton Vocabulary Development project.

Help with writing
Learn-to-type software

Many children with SEN use a keyboard more than other children, so helping them to develop their typing skills is a good idea. There are many programs for this on the market, but two designed specifically for use in education are: 2Type from 2Simple Software and UltraKey 5 from Bytes of Learning.

www.2simple.com
www.bytesoflearning.com

Enhancing word processing

Read & Write from TextHelp and Co:Writer from Don Johnston support children's writing by enhancing existing word processors through predictive text, auditory support, dictionary and thesaurus.

www.texthelp.com
www.donjohnston.com

Accessibility features

Using a computer typically involves typing on a keyboard, using a mouse and reading from the screen. People with visual or mobility impairment may find these operations difficult or impossible to perform. The section on hardware (pages 17–20) suggested a number of products that may help to overcome the difficulties experienced by some children. There are, however, a number of built-in features available on many computers that may provide solutions, or partial solutions to some problems.

Microsoft Windows has a variety of accessibility features. To make best use of these, you will need a PC less than five years old, running Windows XP (or later) and an up-to-date version of Microsoft Office. The features simply need to be switched on and configured, and are then ready for use. A word of warning though: at the time of writing, most of these features are fairly basic, and Microsoft do not recommend them for full-time use. If, for example, you want to have text read to you, there are programs that will do this better than the Microsoft 'Narrator' feature and give you more control over the process. These built-in features do, however, provide an opportunity to experiment with an accessibility feature before investing in a higher quality third-party product to solve a particular problem.

Any of these accessibility settings can be saved for a particular user. This means that each pupil can have their own personal settings which are automatically activated when they log on with their username and password – as is required in Windows.

Below we have listed a number of features that exist in Windows XP. Many can also be found on earlier versions of Windows, although the commands may vary slightly from those described.

To access
'Control Panel':

1 Click on 'Start' on the taskbar.

2 Point to 'Settings'.

Adapting the input
Slowing the pointer
Pupils with poor co-ordination will benefit from having the pointer move more slowly across the screen in relation to the movement of the mouse. To adjust the pointer speed: .

① Click on 'Control Panel'.

② Click on 'Mouse'.

③ Click on 'Pointer Options' tab.

④ Move the slider towards 'Slow'.

⑤ Click on 'OK'.

Enlarging the pointer
Pupils who have trouble seeing the mouse pointer may benefit from increasing the size of the pointer on screen. To make the mouse pointer larger, and hence more visible:

① Click on 'Control Panel'.

② Click on 'Mouse'.

③ Click on 'Pointers' tab.

④ From the 'Scheme' drop-down menu choose 'extra large'.

⑤ Click on 'OK'.

Steering the mouse with the keyboard
If a pupil finds it impossible to operate a mouse or other pointing device but can use the keyboard, then you could set Windows so that the keyboard controls the mouse. To do this:

① Click on 'Control Panel'.

② Click on 'Accessibility Options'.

③ Click on 'Mouse' tab.

④ Make sure 'Use MouseKeys' is ticked.

⑤ Click on 'OK'.

This makes the mouse pointer steerable by using the numeric keypad on the keyboard. To turn this setting on or off, press **CTRL** + left **SHIFT** + **Num Lock** simultaneously. With this option turned on, you can guide the mouse pointer around the screen with the arrow keys on the numeric keypad, and click the mouse button by pressing **5**.

Changing the way the keyboard works

Pupils who find typing difficult because of reduced finger mobility may benefit from one of three settings that change the way the keyboard works:

○ *Ignore repeated keystrokes.* A common problem for people who cannot move their fingers very fast is that they hold down the keys for too long and therefore type repeated letters. It is possible to set the computer so that no matter how long a key is held down, it produces only one letter on screen. Activate this feature in this way:

   ① Click on 'Control Panel'.

   ② Click on 'Accessibility Options'.

   ③ Make sure you are in 'Keyboard' tab.

   ④ Make sure 'Use FilterKeys' option is ticked.

   ⑤ Click on 'Settings'.

   ⑥ Make sure 'Ignore repeated keystrokes' option is selected.

   ⑦ Click on 'OK' to exit both open windows.

○ *Ignore very brief keystrokes.* Pupils with decreased motor control may accidentally press a key when they are trying to press another key. It is possible to set the computer so that key presses are only registered if the key is held down for a longer period. To activate this feature, follow the instructions given above for ignoring repeated keystrokes, but select the 'Ignore quick keystrokes' option instead. Click on 'Settings' and choose the time in seconds that you require from the 'SlowKeys' drop-down menu. You may need to experiment with the time delay to suit different children.

○ *One-handed use.* Some pupils who cannot use both hands at once or have limited dexterity in their fingers may find it difficult to hold down more than one key at a time. It is possible to set up the computer so the pupil can press the **SHIFT**, **CTRL**, **ALT** or 'Windows' key and have it remain active until another key is pressed. To enable this feature:

   ① Click on 'Control Panel'.

   ② Click on 'Accessibility Options'.

   ③ Make sure you are in 'Keyboard' tab.

④ Make sure 'Use StickyKeys' option is ticked.

⑤ Click on 'OK'.

Typing using a pointing device

To access 'Programs':

Click on 'Start' on the taskbar.

If a pupil can operate the mouse or other pointing device but not the keyboard, it is possible for them to type by clicking on an on-screen representation of the keyboard. This option is accessed by choosing the following file path:

① Point to 'Programs'.

② Point to 'Accessories'.

③ Point to 'Accessibility'.

④ Click on 'On-Screen Keyboard'.

This will work with any kind of pointing device, and can be used to type into any program.

Using speech recognition

If a pupil is unable to type or use a pointing device, they may still be able to operate a computer using their voice. Windows XP comes with a built-in speech-recognition system, which works surprisingly well once it is set up properly. You will get the best results with a high quality microphone on a headset so it is near the user's mouth at all times. You will first need to attach a microphone to the computer, then run through a set-up wizard to configure the microphone and the speech-to-text engine. The speech recognition engine has to be 'trained' to recognise a particular voice; the more training it is given, the better it works.

The speech recognition system is accessed through the 'Language Bar', which may or may not be visible on your computer.

① Click on 'Control Panel'.

② Click on 'Regional and Language Options'.

③ Click on 'Languages' tab.

④ Click on 'Details'.

⑤ Make sure you are in 'Settings' tab.

⑥ Click on 'Language Bar'.

⑦ Make sure 'Show the Language bar on the desktop' is ticked.

⑧ Click on 'OK' to exit all open windows.

This displays the language bar on-screen. On the language bar you must click on the microphone icon to start the speech-to-text process. Once you have this facility set up, the pupil can 'type' into any document by simply talking. They can also give commands to save files, close applications and so on.

Adapting the screen

High-Contrast mode

For pupils who are visually impaired or colour-blind, one of the simplest and easiest improvements is to switch Windows XP into High-Contrast mode. This makes on-screen fonts larger and removes distracting colours so that all text is written in bright letters on a dark background. Here is a web page viewed in High-Contrast mode.

To enter High-Contrast mode:

① Click on 'Control Panel'.

② Click on 'Accessibility Options'.

③ Click on 'Display' tab.

④ Tick 'Use High Contrast'.

⑤ Click on 'OK'.

Alternatively, you may use the shortcut option to turn this mode on or off: hold down **ALT**, left **SHIFT** and **PRINT SCREEN** simultaneously. The default settings may not be to your liking, but further configuration options are available. Once you have ticked the 'Use High Contrast' box, as in Step 4 above, you can click on 'Settings' and then choose a colour scheme from the drop-down menu under 'High contrast appearance scheme'.

Enlarging the text

There are various ways to change the size and appearance of the text for users with visual difficulties. Change the default Windows settings for font sizes and background and foreground colours as follows:

① Click on 'Control Panel'.

② Click on 'Display'.

③ Click on 'Appearance' tab.

④ Click on 'Extra Large Fonts' from the drop-down menu under 'Font size'.

⑤ Ensure 'Windows Classic style' is selected under 'Windows and buttons' to access the largest range of colour schemes. Click on your chosen colour scheme from the drop-down menu under 'Colour scheme'.

⑥ Click on 'OK'.

You can also change the font sizes used within word-processing programs and in other applications. In Internet Explorer, for example, click on 'View' in the top menu bar, then select 'Text Size' from the drop-down menu to make the font larger or smaller. Here is a screen with the size set to 'Largest'.

Alternatively, most programs offer the facility to zoom in or out on the whole page so that text appears larger. In Word or Excel, for example, click on 'View' in the top menu bar, click on 'Zoom' from the drop-down menu and then choose a zoom percentage.

Magnifying sections of the screen

Windows XP includes an on-screen magnifier which enlarges a selected area of the screen. It is not the easiest feature to use, but may be useful in certain circumstances.

① Point to 'Programs'.

② Point to 'Accessories'.

③ Point to 'Accessibility'.

④ Click on 'Magnifier'.

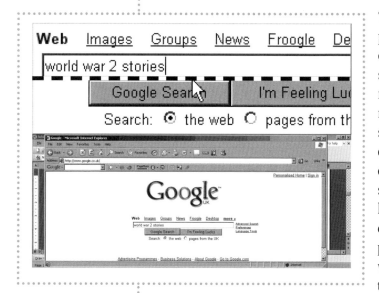

The default settings are not particularly helpful, but there are options for choosing the amount of screen used as a magnifier and the magnification factor. By default the magnifier occupies only a fifth of the screen. Stretch the magnifier area to enlarge it by dragging the bottom edge of the magnified area down the screen. This is shown on the dotted line in the picture. The cursor will change as shown when you have placed it in the right position. In this web page the magnifier is operating in the top half of the screen.

Screen reading

For pupils who cannot see the screen at all, it is possible to set Windows XP to have text read aloud. The feature is called Narrator, and it can read aloud any text that appears on screen, including web pages, documents, and the characters that you type on the keyboard. Narrator can be found as follows:

① Point to 'Programs'.

② Point to 'Accessories'.

③ Point to 'Accessibility'.

④ Click on 'Narrator'.

www.microsoft.com/enable
http://support.microsoft.com/
kb/306902

The built-in Narrator does, unfortunately, have a very artificial-sounding voice with an American accent, but improved voices can be downloaded from the Microsoft website. You may want to try the Microsoft Help and Support website for more information about setting up Narrator to suit your needs.

Chapter 3
Using an interactive whiteboard

A teacher once described the interactive whiteboard (IWB) as 'a magnet for children's eyes', and that is very much how they can seem on a wall in the classroom. Moreover, teachers using them suggest that the effect does not wear off quickly. In this chapter we shall look at ways of using an IWB that will contribute positively to teaching and learning for all children in the class, focusing in particular on some of the issues that you should consider when using IWBs with those with SEN.

The benefits for children with SEN

Teachers observe that IWBs can be especially engaging and motivating for children with special needs as well as those who often choose not to take part in whole-class activities. They can see the effect of their work immediately – and it is very large and in colour. And because all children share the same view, everyone can see exactly what is going on, which makes it especially effective for teaching processes or skills.

IWBs can be especially engaging and motivating for children with special needs.

Several teachers report spectacular initial results with children with attention deficit disorder and those on the autistic spectrum; the highly visual nature of the tasks seems to attract their attention and keeps them attentive in ways that tasks presented at a desk do not.

One of the strengths of the IWB is that you can use the tools as you work with the screen of information, whether it is from published software or whether it is a page you have created. This facility allows children to explore ideas and work together using visual materials, which means those with SEN can demonstrate their abilities without needing to use the written word extensively. There is evidence that this may be a particularly valuable aspect of using an IWB. Many teachers report that children who usually have low self-esteem about their abilities in many literacy and numeracy tasks overcome their sense of failure through working collaboratively at an IWB.

Food for thought
You have to do it, not the teacher telling you. You have to use your brain and think for yourself.

Eight-year-old pupil on using an IWB

Most importantly, IWBs work very effectively with a mixed-ability class, allowing each child to contribute and show what they can do through interacting with the material on the board and with the rest of the class.

Types of IWB

Whilst IWBs are made by various manufacturers, each of whom offers software with slightly different features, the overall experience of use tends to be similar. Perhaps the biggest difference between the types of IWB lies in whether a special pen is needed to operate the board or whether it will allow you to use a finger. Some children need to use their finger to point, so IWBs that can be operated by finger are clearly going to be better for them. This sort of whiteboard can be thought of as a large touch screen: the child can touch an object – whether image, word or number – and move it simply by moving their finger. As children do not need to pick up a special pen to use the board, this can also speed up the process of children taking turns to use it.

Physical considerations
Positioning the IWB
Where best to position your IWB can be a tricky problem and inevitably involves some degree of compromise. Clearly if you want very young or very small children, or children in wheelchairs, to be able to reach the board, then it needs to be positioned at a reasonably low level. However, for adults who will need to use it while standing, a low-level board might be awkward and even create back problems. It may also not be sufficiently visible from all parts of the room. Furthermore, a low-mounted board with a projector mounted on a high ceiling is probably going to result in some image distortion. If the board is installed in a higher position, you should not, for health and safety reasons, allow children to stand on a plinth to reach it. You may have no control over the height of your IWB, but ideally you should discuss these issues with the person installing the board, with the aim of reaching the most appropriate compromise for your situation. Happily, some boards now have height adjustment, allowing you to vary the height according to the needs of the situation.

Another important consideration is the lighting in the room. Light shining directly onto the board affects the visibility. If you need to turn classroom lighting off when you are using the board, remember to turn it back on again when you have finished. Unwanted daylight is best kept out with vertical blinds rather than horizontal ones.

The computer you use to control the IWB can be placed on a nearby desk. If you are going to use it to enter text, then you need to make sure it is positioned so that you can see the class whilst you do so. Wireless technology is now making it easier to communicate with IWBs, and a tablet PC or a wireless keyboard can allow children anywhere in the class to enter data to appear on the board. This helps children with restricted mobility to access the board and ensures that all children, wherever they are in the room, can contribute.

Positioning children
Young children often sit on the floor to look at the IWB, and if they are close to the board then they should sit directly in front of it. If children are sitting in their seats around the class, and therefore further from the board, then you should ensure that all have a clear view. Any child with a hearing or visual difficulty should sit centrally and directly in front of the board, ensuring that they have a good view and that any sound will be received by both ears.

Working with the IWB

Using the screen

Like a computer, the IWB has its own set of tools and settings that alter the appearance of the presentation on the board. It is worth experimenting with these in order to make it as easy as possible for children to view – particularly when you are using your own materials rather than commercially produced software. The following can all be adjusted:

- **Colour** – it may help if the background colour is a pastel shade rather than white. Some children find it easier to read yellow or white text on a black background. Avoid reds and greens as many people have visual difficulty with these colours.

- **Text size** – ensure that the text is large enough to view from the back of the area where the children are sitting, whether around the room or on the floor.

- **Fonts** – choosing a clear font is especially important – Arial, Comic Sans or Sassoon are used in printed materials for primary schools because they are easy to read.

- **Page size** – try to avoid having scrolling text and scrolling pages. When you are making your own resources it is better to make several pages without scrolling than a single page with scrolling.

- **Toolbars** – these can take up a lot of screen space and make it necessary to scroll the page. Often there are toolbars that you do not need for the activity in hand, and you can remove these by pressing the function key **F11**. If you want them back, simply press **F11** again. If children need to use a toolbar for a particular activity, ensure it is placed where they can reach it easily.

Using the touch-screen facility

Kinaesthetic learners find being able to touch elements of the image on the board very helpful. This is particularly the case when reinforcing the language associated with the movement and position: 'is the same as', 'after', 'behind', 'in front', 'next', and so on. The size of the screen means that the movements you ask the children to make can be quite large, and this appears to reinforce learning very effectively.

This experience can be offered both to individuals and to groups of children. Modelling behaviour with the whole class and then allowing the group for whom this approach is especially helpful to work on the board can be a very positive experience. Bear in mind that as children get closer to the board, their field of vision will reduce, and they will no longer be able to see the whole board as they are working. This can influence how you group objects on the board when you want children to interact with them.

Using the board for differentiation

An effective way of differentiating a task is to ask an appropriate question when an individual child comes to the board. The fact that they are always asked an easy question is unlikely to be apparent to the child, and is rarely commented on by other children. That child is then more likely to feel part of the overall activity.

A screen laid out as shown below could be used for a variety of tasks. Each ellipse is labelled with a word or number and is set to capture a number of items (which could be words or pictures). The task is then to drag items from the box into the right ellipse. You can invite individual children to come and do this, adjusting the prompt question to suit each child. Differentiating questions in this way allows everyone to take part, and gives everyone opportunities for showing what they can do.

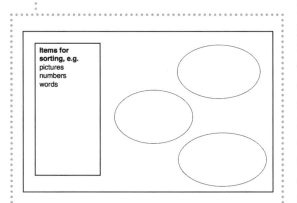

Items for sorting, e.g.
pictures
numbers
words

Using sound

Many of the programs that you might want to use with the whole class will have audio elements – which might be speech, music or sound effects. Whilst all IWBs do have integral sound systems, adding speakers either side of the board will improve the quality significantly and help all children, but especially those with learning difficulties.

It is very important to set the volume so that output is not distorted when sound files are played. Experiment with the volume control on the speakers to get the level right. There are also controls on the computer which can be reached as follows:

① Click on 'Control Panel'.

② Click on 'Sounds and Audio Devices'.

③ Make sure you are in the 'Volume' tab.

④ Move the volume slider up or down as desired.

⑤ Make sure 'Place volume icon in the taskbar' is ticked. The volume icon will then appear on the taskbar so you can quickly adjust the volume as necessary for different pieces of software.

⑥ Click on 'OK'.

If you have a child in your class with hearing loss, you may want to investigate whether the speakers can be linked to the child's hearing aid.

One unavoidable problem with an IWB is that the fan inside the projector can be quite noisy, and this may cause difficulties for some children. Try to seat any children with hearing difficulties so that they can hear both you and the system speakers over the fan noise. This is an important consideration and it may take some experimentation to get it right. And of course, it's a very good idea to switch the projector off when you are not using it – and enjoy the silence!

Using folders

Many teachers create folders of materials on their laptops to use on the IWB. The folder might contain web addresses or names of files with prepared documents or presentations. The folders can be labelled with the date, the lesson or the subject and topic – using whatever system suits you. Some children find it very helpful if this list of resources in the folder is displayed on the screen during the lesson, as it helps them to know where they are and what material is being covered.

Resources for the IWB
Commercial software

Almost all commercial software can be used on an IWB, but the content of some software is more appropriate for the whole-class context than others. As well as being relevant to the lesson, any software used on the IWB needs to be easy to use, have an uncluttered interface and encourage independence. Many of the criteria for selecting software for SEN listed on pages 21–22 and 25–26 will be relevant to software for the IWB.

IWBs offer a wonderful means of displaying and interacting with a rich variety of curriculum-content materials, and they are also an extremely good way for children to learn how to use tools, which can be anything from word processors to drawing packages.

Case study

IWBs add a whole new dimension to the use of art software. Freed from the cognitive load of having to use the mouse, kids' creativity runs riot. Kids who would struggle to make even the simplest of pictures with a mouse confidently choose colours and tools and produce quite complex patterns and pictures with hands and fingers.

In our school we use a programme called Dazzle, which is totally configurable, allowing the teacher to choose which tools will be available on the toolbar. Colours can be chosen from a simple palette of eight up to a complex palette of 255, and menus can be turned off to discourage 'fiddling'. All of the settings can be saved as profiles and simply loaded in when the student returns to the computer. Teachers can choose from a wide variety of tools including basic shapes, fills, tinting and symmetry. You can also import clip art to use as 'stamps' so kids can still create pictures simply by touching the screen.

Primary school teacher

Children's work

Having their work displayed on the IWB for the whole class to see can be very motivating for some children. This could be work on paper which you have scanned or it could be work done on a computer. In some classes, wireless laptops are connected to the IWB, which means the teacher can select the work of different children to display. In classes where that is not possible, the teacher can log on to individual pupils' accounts using the IWB PC, then select work to show.

In some classrooms, tablet PCs are set up to work with the IWB, which allows individual children to contribute text or manipulate the images on the board from their seat in the classroom. Other classes achieve similar results with a wireless keyboard which can be passed around the class for individuals to use. The advantage of both these arrangements is that children who choose not to come to the front of the class, or who are physically not able to do so, can contribute from their seat.

Photographs of activities

One of the most valuable uses of the IWB for children with learning difficulties is perhaps the display of digital photographs of outings or activities in which they have taken part. These images facilitate recall and discussion of the event and encourage children to describe their particular view of it to the rest of the class. Several images could be assembled into a presentation, perhaps together with some writing or a recording of a commentary produced by the children.

Symbols

If you have a child in the class who is using symbols for communication, adding these to the board and allowing the child to use them to communicate with the class will add considerably to their feeling of belonging; it can also help to develop the communication skills of the class as a whole. It is important to put the symbols somewhere on the screen where the child can use them. Do be sensitive, however, to the impression created: if words are always big and in the middle and at the top, then these will tend to be seen as the important elements. Occasionally putting symbols at the top of the screen may help to redress this balance.

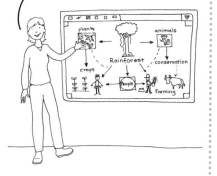

Here's one I prepared earlier!

Recap

The software that comes with the IWB allows you to capture and save any screen. This means that you can save screens used or created during a lesson for recap in another lesson. Starting the next lesson with the same visual stimulus as was used in the previous one can help children to build up connections between one set of ideas and another, and to see the work in context. For children with SEN, this can be especially helpful.

Video

More and more video clips created specifically for educational purposes are becoming available. Using a short video sequence that introduces or sums up a concept, or reinforces an idea through music, can enhance learning for all children, but it is often especially effective for those with special learning needs. If you are using video within a piece of software that offers a whole-screen view, choosing this option ensures that nothing else on the screen will divert the attention away from the moving image.

If you have a video camera to use in class, the sequences you create will be especially meaningful to the children who have been involved in making it. Sometimes, video can offer the least able children, who would otherwise not have a way of presenting their work, to share what they have done with the class. This can result in considerable gains in terms of self-esteem – which will have a knock-on effect in other classroom activities.

Digital microscopes

Digital microscopes can be linked to your computer and the images displayed on the IWB. This offers a way of sharing amongst the whole class an image that previously could be seen by only one child at a time. It may be helpful for children with SEN to help set up the microscope so that they understand the relationship between the object that is being viewed and the image on the screen. Feathers, leaves, a piece of skin or a hair can all make good objects for viewing.

You might invite some children to draw around the coloured image on the IWB. This can be a very useful way of showing many children – not just those with SEN – how diagrams relate to reality: when the microscope image is removed, the drawing they have created will still be there.

Chapter 4
Meeting the needs of children

For all children with SEN, ICT should be an integrated element of the child's individual education programme (IEP). Ideally this should draw on a school-based assessment of the child's ICT requirements, to include recommendations for hardware, software and peripherals or other devices that will enhance the child's ability to participate in classroom activities and help them to integrate both within the school and within the wider community. It is also important to assess what support the child might need. Teaching assistants or parents can play a valuable role here, but may need specific training in the use of the chosen resources.

Looking for an ICT resource on the basis of the pupil's disability may not provide the best solution.

There are numerous ways in which ICT can be useful to pupils with special needs – whether they have physical, emotional or learning difficulties. In this chapter, we look at some very broad categories of special need and, drawing heavily on the experience of classroom teachers, make some suggestions for ICT resources that may be helpful in each category.

Learning difficulties

The term 'learning difficulties' is used here to include children who have moderate learning difficulties, specific learning difficulties such as dyspraxia, severe learning difficulties and profound and multiple learning difficulties. When trying to decide how to use ICT to support a pupil with learning difficulties it is probably better to look at what they are able to do than at what they have difficulty with. Looking for an ICT resource on the basis of the pupil's disability may not provide the best solution.

Case study
Roberto and Sibella, two children with speech delay, sat at the computer together. As they took turns building up vehicles and animals, they repeatedly looked at each other, smiling and sharing enjoyment without needing words. This experience led them to seek each other out for other non-verbal play and the friendship eventually helped them both with their speech as they engaged in more complex games, such as role-play, together.

ICT resources
Literacy
○ **Talking cards.** Talk and record postcards are great for children who can't remember instructions. They can, for example, press the card to hear 'wash your hands' after going to the toilet. They can also be used for sight vocabulary or for sequencing so children can hear a story.
Try: Talktime Recordable Postcards (TTS Group)

○ **Interactive books.** These programs with animations and sound effects bring books to life for children who find reading taxing. Even non-readers can enjoy hearing the story read to them and they will see each word highlighted as it is read.

www.4mation.co.uk
www.oup.com/oxed/primary
www.donjohnston.com
www.riverdeep.net
www.nelsonthornes.com

www.resourcekt.co.uk
www.ldalearning.com
www.inclusive.co.uk
www.widgit.com
www.scion.org.uk

www.edtech.ie
www.inclusive.co.uk
www.wordshark.co.uk

www.thecatchupproject.org
www.lexialearning.com
www.mcgraw-hill.co.uk
www.dyslexiaaction.org.uk
www.resourcekt.co.uk

www.prim-ed.com
www.semerc.com
www.topologika.com

Try: Spinout Stories (4mation); Oxford Reading Tree Talking Stories (Oxford University Press); Start-to-Finish Library (Don Johnston); Living Books® Library (Riverdeep); Wellington Square levelled books (Nelson Thornes)

○ **Literacy skills reinforcement.** There are many programs available to help develop and reinforce literacy skills through repetition and practice. Areas covered include these:

○ Early literacy skills

Try: Animal Match (Resource Education); LDA Language Cards (LDA); Teddy Games (Inclusive Technology); Making Tracks to Literacy (Widgit); Leaps and Bounds (Scion)

○ Sight-word recognition

Try: All My Words (Edtech); Flash! Pro 2 (Inclusive Technology); Wordshark (White Space)

○ Phonological skills

Try: Catch Up Programme (Catch Up); Lexia (Lexia); Sounds Great (McGraw-Hill); Units of Sound (Dyslexia Action); WordWork 1 and 2 (Resource Education)

○ Reading comprehension

Try: Reading for Literacy (Prim-Ed Publishing); Twisted Tales (SEMERC); Sellardore Tales (Topologika)

○ **Scanner and screen-reading software.** Used together, a scanner and a comprehensive screen-reading package can make even very slow readers self-sufficient. Almost any printed material can be scanned in and reproduced on the computer screen; programs will also read web pages from the Internet. Words, sentences or whole sections of text can be spoken and the speed of reading varied. The child can also have words and letters spoken as they are typed, allowing them to spot mistakes as they go along.

www.texthelp.com

Try: Read & Write GOLD (Texthelp)

○ **Spelling.** Spelling exercises can be dull and boring. But presented as games with sound and animation, they become more enjoyable for most learners. Most spelling programs provide immediate feedback, and reward for correct answers – which can be very motivating for those with learning difficulties. Most programs can be geared to the child's level, and can provide diagnosis and records of progress.

www.fishermarriott.com
www.wordshark.co.uk

Try: Starspell (Fisher Marriott); Wordshark (White Space)

○ **Voice-recognition software.** When the child dictates into a microphone linked to the computer, the software converts the speech into written text. This can help children whose abilities with oral language exceed their abilities with written language.

www.nuance.com/
naturallyspeaking
www.nuance.co.uk/viavoice

Try: Dragon Naturally Speaking, Via Voice (Nuance)

○ **Word processing.** A word-processing program offers many benefits for a child with learning difficulties:

○ It allows the child to concentrate initially on their thoughts and ideas; sequencing the thoughts and ideas, word choice, spelling, grammar and punctuation can be attended to afterwards.

○ Words, sentences and paragraphs can easily be added, removed or moved about and edited.

- Built-in grammar and spellcheckers give immediate feedback. Dictionary and thesaurus programs can help children refine their word choice and find the exact word they want.
- Word-processing programs with built-in speech synthesisers can read back text to the child, which can assist with correcting spelling and grammar, and with conveying the intended meaning.
- Some word processors come with a word-bank facility which allows the teacher to set up lists of words. These might comprise, for example, words with which the child has particular difficulty; topic vocabulary; lists of nouns, verbs, adjectives and adverbs; and sentence starters. To hear a word read, the child can point to it with the mouse; clicking on it will import it into the writing.
- Some programs allow images to be incorporated into the document. This can help children choose images to represent their ideas and help them rehearse what they want to say before they start to type in the words.
- Word-prediction programs run in conjunction with a word-processing program and can help with word recall and spelling.
- **Typing skills.** Children who use a keyboard regularly for writing may find it beneficial to improve their keyboarding skills. There are several programs that offer a combination of typing and spelling activities to support children's writing development.

www.ttrs.co.uk
www.bytesoflearning.com
www.2simple.com

Try: Touch-type Read and Spell; UltraKey 5 (Bytes of Learning); 2Type (2simple Software)

Mathematics and numeracy

In mathematics, ICT can be used to:

- develop specific aspects of number theory;
- sharpen calculation skills;
- aid mental recall of number facts in an enjoyable way;
- extend what has been taught in class.

www.logo.com
www.riverdeep-learning.co.uk
www.wordshark.co.uk

Try: BBC Maths Workshop Series (Logotron); Millie's Math House (Riverdeep Interactive Learning); NumberShark (White Space)

Case study

Nicola had cognitive and attention difficulties and found counting with correspondence very difficult. Using simple counting programs such as Wizit Number Fun and Percy was part of a multiactivity approach which gave her the repetition and variety of counting experiences she needed. TAs found it quick and easy to change the options on the programs to a level suitable for her, while letting her use the same game as the other children.

Multimedia

Multimedia authoring programs allow the user to create multimedia projects incorporating text, graphics, sounds, video clips and animations. Children can use their creativity to write their own talking storybooks, presentations and websites, working independently or collaboratively with their peers.

www.indigolearning.com

Try: Centre Stage (Indigo Learning)

Case study

Anna is a Year 6 child with a severe expressive speech and language disorder and poor reading and recording skills. Her comprehension is at a higher level than these other skills, and Anna gets very frustrated with herself when she cannot find the words she wants or is unable to write her ideas down. She often gives up and does not volunteer answers in class. The Writing with Symbols program was used with Anna to make simple reading books and to help her record basic sentences. It made a great difference. Suddenly, she could read word-for-word instead of guessing, and could access a wordlist to record independently.

Dyslexia

ICT can help dyslexic children reach their potential, in particular through providing activities that support appropriate learning styles. Software to support learners with dyslexia can be divided into two categories: programs to help and support children with writing, recording and reading; and programs to provide opportunities for learning and practising skills.

ICT resources

Identification

ICT can be a valuable tool for diagnosis and assessment. Lucid Research at the University of Hull provides a quick and reliable online screening for dyslexia. They also offer tools for more detailed analysis.

www.lucid-research.com

Literacy

Computers are helpful to dyslexic children in that they provide an automatic left–right orientation for reading and writing. There is a wide range of software available for specific literacy activities that will be helpful to dyslexic children as well as to those with general reading difficulties.

- **Spelling.** There are many different programs that provide multisensory support for developing spelling skills – from games to reinforce particular spelling rules through to complete teaching schemes.
Try: Wordshark (White Space); Nessy Learning Programme (Nessy); Starspell (Fisher Marriott Software)

www.wordshark.co.uk
www.nessy.co.uk
www.fishermariott.com

- **Interactive books.** With animation, sound effects and text highlighted as it is read aloud, interactive books can allow dyslexic children who struggle with reading to have the same access to books as their peers. More and more books are being published in e-book formats, and some classics are available for free download.
Try: Spin out Stories (4mation); Oxford Reading Tree Talking Stories (Oxford University Press); Start-to-Finish Library (Don Johnston); Living Books® Library (Riverdeep); Wellington Square levelled books (Nelson Thornes)

www.4mation.co.uk
www.oup.com/oxed/primary
www.donjohnston.com
www.riverdeep.net
www.nelsonthornes.com

- **AcceleRead AcceleWrite (Iansyst).** This is a popular teaching program which uses speech feedback to accelerate reading development.

www.iansyst.co.uk

- **Specific reading skills programs.** There is a wide range of resources that focus on the development of specific reading skills, and teachers can choose those that utilise appropriate learning styles.
Try: Eye Track and Phoneme Track (SEMERC) – to work on the visual and auditory processing skills involved with reading; and RocketReader (RocketReader) – to improve reading speed and develop strategies for scan reading.

www.semerc.com
www.rocketreader.com
www.dyslexic.com

◔ **Word processing**. Children with dyslexia often have a very clear idea of what they want to write, but the process of turning those ideas into the written word can be very frustrating. Word processors that offer a predictive-text function, intelligent spellcheckers and text-to-speech options will all provide useful support.
Try: Clicker 5 (Crick Software); Read & Write GOLD (TextHelp); SOLO, Co:Writer (Don Johnston)

www.cricksoft.com
www.texthelp.com
www.donjohnston.com

◔ **Voice recognition software**. Speech-to-text programs do require some training but they offer the child the great reward of producing text that others can read – which may be highly motivating for the dyslexic child for whom that experience is rare.
Try: Dragon Naturally Speaking, Via Voice (Nuance)

www.nuance.com/
naturallyspeaking
www.nuance.co.uk/viavoice

◔ **Mind-mapping**. This technique has proved useful for dyslexic learners to help shape their thinking and to provide a structure for writing. Mind-mapping software can be a good tool for getting children started on a piece of work by brainstorming and building up their ideas. Words added to the mind map can usually be transferred to a sequential text format, allowing children to start writing from the words they already recognise. Mind maps can be used across the curriculum and as an effective teaching tool on an IWB.
Try: Textease IdeasMap (Softease); Kidspiration, Inspiration (TAG Learning)

www.softease.co.uk
www.taglearning.com

◔ **Typing skills**. Children with dyslexia often benefit from improving their keyboarding skills. There are several programs that offer a combination of typing and spelling activities to support children's writing development.
Try: Touch-type Read and Spell; UltraKey 5 (Bytes of Learning); 2Type (2simple Software)

www.ttrs.co.uk
www.bytesoflearning.com
www.2simple.com

◔ **Portable devices**. There are various portable devices that may help children with dyslexia. In particular, electronic dictionaries and thesauri will give them the confidence that they have found the right word and can spell it. Check the reliability and level before investing. Reading pens that scan printed words and read them aloud can also provide useful support.

Mathematics and numeracy

Research shows that many children with dyslexia struggle with their numeracy skills. A calculator can be a useful aid, not only for getting a correct answer, but also for learning particular products or number bonds and for encouraging the estimation of answers. Spreadsheets can help students to record their work and give good examples of layout.

Many mathematics programs rely heavily on reading skills, but some offer the support of audio instructions. One of these is Numbershark (White Space), widely used with children who have language difficulties because it develops maths skills through games.

www.wordshark.co.uk
www.orbeducation.com
www.2simple.com
www.ltscotland.org.uk/
edresources/software
www.fishermariott.com

Try also: Times Tables (Orb Education); 2Calculate (2simple Software); LifeSkills: Time and Money (Learning & Teaching Scotland); StarFractions (Fisher Marriott Sofware)

Autistic spectrum disorders

No two children with an autistic spectrum disorder (ASD) are alike. Children may have varying degrees of difficulties associated with their ASD, and many have other associated learning disabilities. It is vital, therefore, when considering the possible use of any ICT resources, to assess the purpose and content in relation to the individual child.

ICT can offer a number of benefits for children with an ASD. For example, many have problems in the areas of interacting with others, communication, organisation and motor skills, and ICT may offer a way of coping with some of these issues. A computer may also provide a refuge, a safe place to work when the hurly burly of classroom life becomes too distressing.

Case study

Aaron was on the autistic spectrum and had difficulty accessing a broad and balanced curriculum. After repeated attempts to attract his attention he showed interest in a very simple cause-and-effect program with a high level of visual and aural reward (SwitchIt Patterns). Over a period of time he learned to sit and use the touch screen for long enough to get the reward. His enjoyment led to more eye contact with adults and encouraged his TAs and teachers to have higher expectations of him.

There are, however, a number of important considerations to bear in mind when using ICT resources with children with ASD.

● The position of the computer in the classroom is important. Some children enjoy working in a secluded environment where they cannot be distracted by other people or things in the classroom, and they may find it helpful to have panels around the computer. Some children may be sensitive to the sounds from the computer or the light from the screen, and may either find these distressing or become distracted by them. If this is the case, the computer may need to be kept out of sight or be screened off in some way.

● Even if the computer is positioned away from the rest of the classroom, ICT should not be allowed to become a means of isolation; rather it should offer one alternative means of communication to be used in conjunction with others. The computer can be a helpful refuge or pacifier, but it is important that it is not used continually to avoid contact with other children.

● Children with ASD may have unusual fixations on objects or parts of objects, rather like a form of tunnel vision. Working on a computer means they are able to focus on the screen and block out other distractions, but care should be taken to ensure that ICT does not become an obsession.

● Children with ASD do not like changes in routine. When any ICT resource is introduced, it should be done gradually and be explained carefully.

● It is always good practice to ensure that new software is installed and tested and that you can use it confidently before introducing it to a child – and this is especially important with software you plan to use for children on the autistic spectrum.

● With children with an ASD, there is always a risk of sensory overstimulation and overindulgence, and this should be borne in mind when selecting software. Take careful account of the graphics, animations and sounds in a program – and the needs of the individual child. Change software on a regular basis to avoid overindulgence and obsession with a particular program.

ICT resources

- **Word-processing programs**. Children with an ASD may experience difficulty with motor skills, and writing can be a difficult and unwelcome exercise. Word-processing programs can help, and it is useful to have one with a built-in speech synthesiser so the child can hear text read back. Word-bank and picture-bank facilities are another worthwhile addition.
- **Word-prediction programs**. To use with word-processing packages.
- **Digital cameras**. These can be useful in helping to remind children about acceptable behaviour. Pictures can be taken of the child exhibiting a desired behaviour, and captions added to form a mini-story. The message is reinforced when these desired actions are read repeatedly with or by the child.

Case study

One boy in Year 5 found word processing easier than handwriting. This made his work legible for his audience and helped him organise his thoughts and time. Working with a TA, he became less frustrated because mistakes were more easily rectified. The spellchecker and thesaurus provided him with a source of additional help. He enjoyed adding pictures to his work for visual clues, and communicated with others by using the word processor to send them notes.

Visual difficulties

Visual impairment can take many forms. Each eye condition will be quite specific and the impact on learning will therefore be different for each child. Difficulty with reading and writing is usually the main barrier to learning, and this may result in lower achievement in literacy, numeracy and other areas. This difficulty may affect a child's motivation and their ability to engage in learning.

If you have a visually impaired child, you will need to consider where they sit in the classroom – probably somewhere close to the front. If you need to turn the lights off when using the IWB, remembering to turn them back on afterwards could be particularly important for such a child. You may also want to consider whether glare-free lighting may help.

Case study

A teacher in a nursery school found that the IWB appeared to be a problem for a particular child. This child was subsequently diagnosed with narrow focal vision, which meant she was unable to focus on the full width of the screen.

A visually impaired child will need a computer screen which is not affected by direct light. A higher quality monitor or a glare-free screen may be necessary for some children. Some of the accessibility features described on pages 26–31 may help visually impaired children.

ICT resources

www.dolphincomputeraccess.com

- **Screen magnification software**. This can be used to adapt the screen display to meet an individual's needs.
  Try: SuperNova, Lunar (Dolphin)

- **Screen-reading software**. Programs that read screen text aloud – as letters, words, sentences or whole sections of the screen – may be of some value. However, the software usually reads only the text in a document and not the menus and system messages. It is therefore of limited value to a visually impaired child who wants to use a computer independently. Some websites will have text descriptions for the graphics used that can be read out using the screen reader, but this information is not always provided.

- **Optical character recognition (OCR) software**. This is usually used in conjunction with a scanner. It reads the text from a page and converts it to digital format which can be imported into your word processor and edited to suit your own needs.

- **Optical Braille recognition software**. This works with a standard flatbed scanner and allows documents in Braille to be scanned and translated into print. Braille translation software converts printed documents on-screen or on a disk to a format which is then embossed on a Braille printer (embosser).

- **Multimedia curriculum software**. Programs using speech and sound alongside bright pictures – often designed for young learners – may motivate visually impaired children to explore and interact with their surroundings.
  Try: SwitchIt! Scenes, SwitchIt! Patterns (Inclusive Technology)

www.inclusive.co.uk

Case study

A child with nystagmus and albinism benefited from having the screen changed to a different colour – in his case, green. He now does his touch typing with his preferred screen colour.

Hearing difficulties

Expectations of achievement for hearing-impaired and deaf children should be the same as for any other children, but it should be borne in mind that they often have difficulty with acquiring language and with communication. All hearing-impaired children make use of additional visual clues – which could be sign language, lip-reading or reading facial expressions. If you have children in your class with a hearing impairment, consider how the room may be arranged to facilitate communication, providing an optimum position for those who need to lip-read or use sign language.

For children who are hearing-impaired, ICT can help with motivation, independence and confidence. It can also be a valuable way to improve communication: working collaboratively on multimedia projects as well as using the Internet, email, text messaging and video conferencing can all help to promote social contact and reduce isolation.

Case study

Sean's local authority provided support in the form of an audio typist who sat at his side in class and typed what was said for Sean to read from a screen. This, however, caused problems. Unlike other children, Sean could not choose where he sat in class or whom he sat next to. If he was part of a group, his typist had to be there too. Other children found the clickety-clack of a keyboard distracting, and so did Sean: because he had to sit very close to the machine, the noise was amplified by his hearing aid.

Sean's peripatetic teacher of the deaf arranged to borrow a wireless screen from the Deaf Children's Communication Aids Project (DCCAP). This worked well, so she applied to the project for Sean to have his own system. DCCAP paid for a laptop and wireless display, a mouse, three sets of batteries and a charger. They also provided the software to link the screen to the laptop.

Now Sean can be part of any group; he sees the class discussion on the screen and can concentrate more easily. When Sean started studying for his GCSEs, CAP supplied Inspiration, a mind-mapping program which is particularly useful for planning out work for pupils with strong visual skills, and a CD writer to make it easier to transfer projects from one machine to another.

Much educational software has an audio element, so programs for the hearing-impaired child need to be carefully selected. Where appropriate, the sound output can be linked to enhanced amplification to aid the child. Sounds become more meaningful when heard in conjunction with moving images on the screen.

ICT resources

◐ Sign-language software. Programs are available to help children learn sign language.
www.waterfallrainbows.co.uk
Try: Sign to Me, Fingerspelling resources (Waterfall Rainbows)

◐ Spelling and word recognition. Hearing-impaired children need programs that take a visual approach.
www.thrass.co.uk
www.wordshark.co.uk
www.camsoftpartners.co.uk
Try: THRASS (Thrass); Wordshark (White Space); Fun with Texts (Camsoft Educational Software)

◐ Writing. Word processors that offer a predictive-text function, intelligent spellcheckers and text-to-speech options will provide useful support.
www.donjohnston.com
Try: Co:Writer (Don Johnston)

◐ Mind-mapping. This visual approach to thinking and planning may suit hearing-impaired children, and mind-mapping software may be a useful tool.
www.taglearning.com
Try: Inspiration (TAG Learning)

◐ Multimedia software. Programs that can combine a variety of resources – video clips, still pictures, text and sound – can provide hearing-impaired children with access to information in an immediate and visual form.
www.indigolearning.com
Try: Centre Stage (Indigo Learning)

Physical difficulties

Children with physical disabilities find gross movements difficult and may also have difficulties with finer movements, or a combination of both. Many cannot write or type; others can do so only at a slow pace and the end result may still be illegible. Some may have visual–perceptual difficulties or impaired speech, or be non-verbal. Access to the curriculum can be difficult, but ICT can play a big role in improving the situation for these children.

Case study

Jake was severely affected by cerebral palsy. He was visually impaired, had no mobility and poor fine-motor skills. He could identify and use a small brightly coloured switch which worked an audio cassette. Every day, he would start and stop his audio tapes. Other children loved to dance to his music, and developed a Simon-Says-type game, in which they stopped moving whenever Jake turned off the tape. In this way, he could be an important member of a group, enjoy spontaneous social play and be independent of adult help.

Peripheral devices and other ICT equipment can be used to compensate for a child's lack of motor control. Computers can help to compensate for the loss of normal means of access to educational resources. A child with physical disabilities may find handling pieces of paper difficult, whereas input and interaction with a computer can be arranged to match their particular abilities. Some children will, with the right support, be able to record or write their work on the computer; some will only be able to 'read' materials that can 'talk'.

It is essential to position equipment safely and in such a way that the child can use it comfortably and alongside their peers. Height-adjustable tables, wrist rests and arm supports can provide additional support. The size of screen and the display on the screen should be such that the child does not have to strain to see it.

Try to ensure the child does not always work on the computer alone but has plenty of opportunities to work with others. Careful positioning of the ICT resources that the child uses can help. Make sure that there is room for the child with physical difficulties to sit alongside one of their peers and that there is space for a TA to support them if required.

ICT resources
Basic skills

- **Switch-accessible cause-and-effect software**. These simple programs help to make children aware of how one action can lead to another; they also teach children with physical disabilities how to use single-click and two-click operations. For example, a face is built up on the screen gradually, by each click of a switch.
  Try: Switch it! Series, Touch Funfair, Smart Alex, Happy Duck, Step-by-Step (all Inclusive Technology); Sensory Software (Sensory Software)

www.inclusive.co.uk
www.sensorysoftware.com

Literacy

- **Interactive books**. These can provide access to reading material, which would otherwise be inaccessible to the child with physical difficulties.
  Try: Oxford Reading Tree Talking Stories(Oxford University Press); Clicker Talking Books (Crick Software); Living Books® Library (Riverdeep); Wellington Square levelled books (Nelson Thornes); Start-to-Finish Library (Don Johnston)

www.oup.com/oxed/primary
www.cricksoft.com
www.riverdeep.net
www.nelsonthornes.com
www.donjohnston.com

◆ **Scanner and screen-reading software**. Used together, a scanner and a comprehensive screen-reading package can make even very slow readers self-sufficient. Almost any printed material can be scanned in and reproduced on the computer screen; programs will also read web pages from the Internet. Words, sentences or whole sections of text can be spoken and the speed of reading varied. The child can also have words and letters spoken as they are typed, allowing them to spot mistakes as they go along.
www.texthelp.com
Try: Read & Write GOLD (TextHelp)

◆ **Word processing**. Word-processing programs enable children with physical difficulties to write and to produce finished work in a state comparable to that produced by their peers. A spellchecker, a grammar and punctuation checker, a dictionary and a thesaurus can all be helpful features. Word-processing programs with inbuilt speech synthesisers that can read back text may also be useful.
www.donjohnston.com
www.softease.com
www.inclusive.com
www.cricksoft.com
Try: Write:Out Loud (Don Johnston); Textease Studio CT (Softease); Inclusive Writer (Inclusive Technology); Clicker 5 (Crick Software)

◆ **Word-prediction software**. Used in conjunction with a word-processing program, this can help with word recall and spelling.
www.donjohnston.com
www.cricksoft.com
Try: Co:Writer (Don Johnston); Penfriend (Crick Software)

◆ **Voice-recognition software**. When the child dictates into a microphone linked to the computer, the software converts the speech into written text.
www.nuance.com/naturallyspeaking
www.nuance.co.uk/viavoice
Try: Dragon Naturally Speaking, Via Voice (Nuance)

Multimedia

◆ Multimedia authoring programs allow the user to create multimedia projects incorporating text, graphics, sounds, video clips and animations. Children can use their creativity to write their own talking story books, presentations and websites, working independently or collaboratively with their peers.
www.taglearning.com
www.riverdeep-learning.co.uk
www.spasoft.co.uk
www.cricksoft.com
www.indigolearning.com
Try: HyperStudio (TAG Learning); Storybook Weaver (Riverdeep Interactive Learning); Storymaker (Spa); Clicker 5 (Crick Software); BuzzWebz, Centre Stage (Indigo Learning)

Art

◆ Many children with physical disabilities have difficulty in manipulating a pen, paintbrush and scissors. Art packages can help them to experience art in a unique and empowering way. They can choose from a wide variety of tools, stamps and colours, and erase errors. Dazzle 03 (Indigo Learning) can be configured to offer the child only the tools you want, and can be used with a graphics tablet to give a physical experience closer to using art
www.indigolearning.com
materials.

Case study

Freddie has cerebral palsy. His fine-motor control skills are poor, making writing very difficult. His speech is also poor, so writing is potentially a powerful way for him to show what he can do. However, his handwriting is slow and results in unclear work that does not reflect the quality of his ideas.

The school provided Freddie with an AlphaSmart Neo, which has a keyboard and small screen. Together with the built-in predictive-text facility, this helps him to get his thoughts down in writing more quickly. Freddie's poor finger control makes typing difficult, so he uses a finger guard to make sure he presses only the key he wants. The machine can be used anywhere, even outside. Freddie also has his own printer, so he can independently print out completed work to go into his exercise book.

When he has finished the content creation he can, if he wishes, plug the machine into a classroom computer and load the text into Word. He can then work on the presentation of his work by changing layout and fonts, adding pictures if appropriate.

The AlphaSmart has made a huge difference to Freddie. With handwriting, he might produce ten lines in an hour; with his AlphaSmart it could be 30 lines. His classmates are usually very impressed. The AlphaSmart is seen as belonging to Freddie and is part of what he has and is, and so it is not seen as an issue that he has one and others do not.

Chapter 5
ICT for SENCos

How ICT can help

The role and responsibilities of the SENCo have grown significantly over the last few years. One result of the recent strategy documents, in particular *Every Child Matters*, the SEN code of practice and *Harnessing Technology*, is that the SENCo's job description now varies according to individual setting and circumstance. As mentioned in Chapter 1, the documents also emphasise the important role of ICT in enabling the SENCo to implement the strategies within the school. The chart overleaf details the ways in which ICT can provide support in relation to the various responsibilities of the SENCo.

This list of responsibilities represents a heavy load for SENCos, particularly in small primary schools where they still have the same breadth of responsibility but for fewer pupils. Setting up ICT systems to support the management of SEN within the school can create the following benefits:

● information on pupils is recorded in a co-ordinated, systematic way;

● accurate, up-to-date information can be quickly retrieved;

● it is easier to analyse results and evaluate the effectiveness of projects and practices;

● time is saved.

Whatever system you put in place, you should ensure that:

● staff are fully trained and feel confident in using it;

● it is kept up to date by all users;

● security is considered and appropriate measures are put in place;

● the system is robust and works all the time.

It is vital to consider the planning, training and support needs for the effective use of ICT resources.

ICT and teaching assistants

A SENCo is responsible for the complex task of matching each child's need with teacher and TA skills and the other resources available. The team of TAs is especially vital for the effective support of SEN children within a school. In a large primary school, there will be many TAs who seek appropriate leadership and management in order to be effective in their role. One SENCo explained that she now managed a team of over twenty teaching assistants, each of whom had some role in supporting children with SEN – either as individuals or through a special learning group. How well TAs are able to use ICT resources therefore plays a crucial role in the effectiveness of SEN provision within the school.

"...ensure the system is robust"

The role of ICT for the SENCo

Area of SENCo responsibility	Examples of responsibilities	Ways in which ICT can provide support
To co-ordinate provision for pupils with SEN	○ Identifying individual pupil needs ○ Contributing to assessment ○ Supporting IEP / Individual Behaviour Plan (IBP) writing ○ Monitoring and reviewing ○ Managing school-based units, e.g. hearing support ○ Monitoring the progress of pupils on the record of concern ○ Ensuring appropriate special arrangements are in place for exams	○ Gathering and storing evidence for pupils on the record of concern ○ Managing correspondence with parties concerned ○ Writing IEPs ○ Storing and managing records for pupils at SA, SA+ and with statements
To contribute to the strategic planning for SEN within the school	○ Drawing up the SEN Action Plan, with input from teachers, TAs and other professionals ○ Ensuring SEN is an integral part of the School Development Plan	○ Sharing information for the development and delivery of plans

To liaise with staff within the school and with outside agencies	○ Internally, these include:
	  • fellow teachers
	  • TAs, support staff
	  • governors
	  • parents
	
	○ Externally, these include:
	  • the local authority (LA)
	  • educational psychologists
	  • parent partnerships
	  • support and advisory services
	  • other schools (for liaising on school transfer)
	  • health professionals, e.g. speech therapist, physiotherapist, occupational therapist, community paediatrician
	  • social services
		○ Delivering a differentiated learning experience through different teaching and learning styles as appropriate
		○ Overcoming barriers to learning
		○ Communicating with teachers running additional programmes
		○ Communicating with other staff, parents, external agencies and the wider team supporting the child
		○ Delivering outreach work
		○ Maintaining accurate and up-to-date records
		○ Giving information about pupils with SEN to supply staff
		○ Arranging, planning and providing administration for meetings
		○ Using the Internet to find information about external services
		○ Communicating with teachers in other schools for advice

The role of ICT for the SENCo

Area of SENCo responsibility	Examples of responsibilities	Ways in which ICT can provide support
To promote staff development in relation to SEN	◗ Keeping oneself informed about current issues in SEN, latest research, available resources, legislation and LA policy through reading, courses, conferences and so on ◗ Ensuring SEN is seen as a whole-school issue ◗ Identifying and prioritising staff training needs ◗ Contributing to INSET ◗ Organising INSET by external specialists ◗ Acting as TA mentor ◗ Facilitating induction for trainee teachers and NQTs	◗ Accessing government documents, which are all published on the Internet, often with links to further useful sites ◗ Accessing the LA site, which provides additional interpretation of government documents as well as information on local policy and resources ◗ Participating in virtual communities and discussion groups that allow the sharing of experiences and expertise ◗ Using online training or supplementary online support
To manage SEN resources	◗ Purchasing, organising and cataloguing resources ◗ Acting as line manager for TAs and the support team ◗ Timetabling and organising deployment of teachers (including the SENCo), TAs and others to teach individuals and small groups and provide in-class support ◗ Managing the training budget ◗ Recruiting and interviewing	◗ Researching resources through online catalogues ◗ Accessing independent evaluation, reviews and advice on quality and relevance of resources ◗ Purchasing resources online ◗ Cataloguing the school's SEN resources ◗ Recording the use and location of expensive equipment ◗ Managing software licensing agreements ◗ Auditing the school resources, keeping track of changes and sharing information in order to make better use of school resources as well as identifying gaps ◗ Managing budgets ◗ Advertising jobs online
To maintain and oversee records of all pupils with SEN	◗ Maintaining the list of pupils at SA, SA+ and with statements ◗ Assisting with Pupil Level Annual School Census (PLASC) records in conjunction with admin. staff ◗ Maintaining dated records of contact with other agencies ◗ Keeping records of relevant information about pupils with SEN ◗ Tracking, monitoring and reviewing individual or group progress ◗ Organising, conducting and reporting on annual reviews and transition reviews	◗ Storing, updating and retrieving information, including: • records of pupil progress; • records of meeting with parents and advisory staff; • reports from outside agencies, e.g. health professionals or child protection

Using ICT resources with children

In supporting any child with SEN, the teacher and TA need to consider how best to support their individual needs, and what role ICT should play in giving that support. The process may be assisted by the following questions:

- Where should the TA sit in relation to the computer or other ICT device?

- What is the relationship between child, computer and adult? For example, it may be necessary for the teacher or TA to set up the software with appropriate options prior to use by the child. This will allow the child to work independently. And the learner may prefer to work alone, or they may prefer to work in collaboration with other children or an adult in order to discuss ideas and responses to the software.

- Is the computer feedback appropriate? Many software programs include feedback, which may be a simple response of 'Correct' or 'Try again', or it may be some form of help to understand how to answer correctly. A TA can observe what children are having difficulty with and can assist the learner who needs additional help.

- How should the TA react when other children want to get involved with an activity involving ICT? It is important that the TA understands the purpose of using the software and is therefore able to decide when it is appropriate for classmates to participate in the learning. They need to watch out for the enthusiastic computer-users who want to take over, but be able also to take advantage when there is a good opportunity for the SEN child to work as part of a team.

When using ICT resources, it is important that the TA understands their role in supporting the child. It may be, for example, that the child has a problem with writing and is being encouraged to learn keyboarding skills. Here, the TA may need to provide little support other than checking at the outset that the child understands what is required, and then keeping an eye on them to ensure they are on task and working at the appropriate level. If, however, the child has more severe difficulties, the TA may need to provide a greater degree of support. With a child who is deaf, for example, the TA may need to sign the instructions.

TA's tip

When children are sitting next to you, you should be at right angles to them, rather than beside. This allows you to see their work and also make eye contact. Also, be aware of whether the child is right or left handed, so that you can sit on the better side from their point of view.

With any ICT resource, the TA – and therefore the child – will always benefit from being given some time to explore the resource for themselves and to become familiar with the way it works. The teacher should also ensure the TA understands what is expected of them before beginning to work alongside the child. A frequent problem is that TAs are not given adequate planning, preparation and assessment (PPA) time, so they have a limited opportunity to do this. This preparation is, however, vital for effective use of resources, and should be taken into account during planning, if at all possible. And involving the TA in planning will often reap greater rewards for the children.

Sometimes, a new ICT resource such as a computer program does not appear to help the child immediately and does not have instant appeal. If this is the case, the TA should be aware of the need for persistence, as it may take a few sessions to get to grips with it and for the child to feel confident.

Communication

Many children become emotionally attached to their TA and develop confidence through the relationship – which can create a problem if the TA then leaves. The transfer to a new TA will be eased if there are accurate records of what has been achieved, and notes about appropriate learning strategies and styles, and what is motivating for the child. Again, if there is a good ICT system for recording and retrieving this information, the whole process will be more efficient and effective.

Each child will be different in their response to ICT resources. For example, one child may become absorbed by a particular computer game; another may respond especially well to the use of a digital camera and be encouraged to communicate. Teachers and staff need to understand what individual children respond to, and to share this information in order to build on each child's strengths and interests. If there are any barriers to learning these should also be communicated. For example, if a child has difficulty in using an IWB or is unable to read small text on a small screen, this needs to be recorded and understood by all staff.

Skills and training

For the SENCo

To use ICT effectively to support you in your role as SENCo, you will need ICT skills. You may already have all the skills you need, or you may feel that you need further training in a specific area or areas, which could include the following:

● **ICT for administration**. It is likely that the software package available to you will be Microsoft Office, which includes the word-processing program Word and the spreadsheet program Excel. It also includes PowerPoint, a presentation program which may be useful when it comes to providing INSET. Many of the skills learned in Office are transferable to other software packages.

● **Using ICT in education**. It is important for the SENCo to know about the appropriate use of computers at school. This includes issues such as the length of time children should spend on a computer, physical requirements for use, security and software options. You will also need to know about the specific requirements of your school and the procedures used.

Ideally your school will provide the necessary support, but if this is not forthcoming, there are a number of other ways to develop your skills:

● you may be able to find colleagues who will help;

● your LA may offer a part-time course or the local FE college may run an evening class;

❍ you may be able to find a relevant online course, although this method of learning does not suit everyone.

For teaching assistants

TAs are usually very effective in their role of supporting children, but experience of and confidence in using ICT tends to vary greatly. For TAs to be effective in supporting children using technology, it is important that they themselves feel confident in its potential and operation.

TAs do not necessarily get the training they need and their work schedule does not generally allow any non-contact time. Moreover, TAs are often part-time employees, which presents additional challenges in keeping them informed, communicating with them as a team and fulfilling their training needs. However, if you are going to make effective use of ICT resources, the training of TAs should be an important consideration in planning. Depending on the type of training required, it could take place either in school from teachers or other TAs, or via external training courses that focus on the needs of TAs. The lack of a computer may also be a barrier for TAs. The majority of teachers have their own personal laptop, but this is not the norm for TAs. Many schools have a 'library' of laptops which TAs can use when required, for example when they need to familiarise themselves with a new piece of software before working alongside the child.

Training in the following areas can be valuable for TAs (and may also be useful for teachers):

● **Interactive whiteboard**. IWBs are widely used in primary schools and can be used effectively by TAs for group work. It is fairly easy to learn to use an IWB, but a brief introductory course focusing on the interactive potential of the board can be very beneficial. TAs can then use the board's features and facilities effectively in a variety of situations and the pupils gain better value from it.

● **Software**. Whilst most educational software packages are fairly intuitive and easy to learn, some, such as software tools, have huge potential that may not be immediately obvious. Training can help both teachers and TAs to understand that potential and get greater value from the software. Training in this type of resource is likely to be a worthwhile investment.

It is worth investigating with the publisher, prior to purchase, if training is needed, and if so at what cost and in what format. For example, Clicker 5 is a popular SEN tool which draws on content generated by the teacher as well as other published resources. The publishers, Crick Software, offer a range of training and support for users of the program, including hands-on training, support training booklets, and visits to one of the regional Clicker Centres.

● **Peripherals and hardware.** This covers a wide variety of resources, and training could be anything from a short course on using videos in education to time allocated to getting to grips with a bespoke piece of kit which has been put together to cater for an individual child.

Funding

Local authorities delegate SEN resources to mainstream schools and have arrangements to delegate additional resources for pupils with the most severe and complex SEN. The provision does vary between LAs and between schools. At a school level, there are tensions about how best to allocate the funding, with the challenge of ICT resources and people being heavy costs.

Case study

Only one TA is actually fully funded for a statemented child. If I get to the stage of a child's needs being so severe that a statement is necessary, a place at a specialised learning centre is usually found.

All TAs have training in ICT but it is so broad you could not train for everything or every need that may arise. We had training from the local authority inclusion service but, again, I had to fund the extra hours for training.

SENCo

Partnership with parents

One of the SENCo's areas of responsibility is liaison with parents or carers of children with SEN, to share information, discuss progress, agree targets and seek constructive ways of reinforcing learning at home.

Using ICT at home

In working with parents, consideration should be given to ways in which ICT can be used at home to support and enhance what the child is doing with ICT in school. The following questions may provide a useful starting point:

- Is there a computer at home that the child can use? If so, does it operate in the same way as the school computer? If not, could the school lend a laptop for home use?

- If the child uses an input device, can one be provided at home; or can the school one be taken home?

- Does the child need any other specialist equipment? Children may benefit from taking some equipment home. Whether this is permissible will depend on who owns the equipment, how many children use it, and its portability and value. If equipment is being taken home, then check the school's insurance policy and make clear to the parent who is responsible for it should it be stolen or anything go wrong.

- Can the software the child uses at school be used at home as well? This will depend on the terms of the software licence. Increasingly software publishers allow use of software at home, but you will need to check. It may be that the parents have to purchase an additional licence for home use.

- Can the child access school work from home in order to continue working on it? There are several ways to do this. It may be possible for children at home to access their personal files on the school server; this will depend on the software and on your school system. Or it may be possible to launch work to the Internet or email it home. Alternatively, memory sticks can be used for transferring work, but there is a risk of their being lost or forgotten.

You should consider what information parents need in order to support their child effectively. It is worth spending time explaining the learning objectives, how to operate the equipment and how to get the best out of it. Parents will then be more confident in offering support and working as part of the learning team.

Support for parents

Parents can often feel isolated when their child is identified as having special needs. ICT can assist greatly in providing help and support. As the SENCo, your role includes:

- ● keeping them up to date with their child's progress and learning – the most efficient way of doing this is through maintaining regular email contact between meetings;
- ● putting them in touch with other parents in a similar situation;
- ● offering specialist advice, which could include providing a list of useful websites;
- ● informing them of appropriate virtual networks which might provide support;
- ● advising them of available software and resources which may help their child (including free as well as paid-for resources, if possible).

Training parents

Consider what parents need to know and offer them some free training. This will make them more confident and build a more effective partnership. If you consider it too time-consuming to train all parents, you might consider an alternative strategy in which you select and train a few parents, who then become trainers for other parents. Sessions might cover, for example, managing computer resources at home, what to do about security, the physical positioning of the computer, and the role of the parent in the learning process. Make the sessions practical, engaging and non-threatening and you will gain their support.

Financial support

Some support has been offered to children through the Communication Aids Project (CAP) which ran from 1 April 2002 to 31 March 2006. It received £5 million a year and was funded by the DfES. It was aimed at supporting pupils, in partnership with schools and LAs, by first identifying individual needs, and then helping to supply equipment to meet those needs.

The equipment was owned by the project, but it is hoped that the equipment ownership will transfer to the children who have benefited from it. If children are using this equipment at home, it is advisable that parents are trained in its use, understand its purpose and are aware of insurance, warranty and maintenance issues.

www.capclub.co.uk/games.php

The CAP website was developed and managed by Becta. Although this site is no longer being updated, there is still some valuable contact information on it plus some fun games for children.

VAT relief

Suppliers usually have to charge VAT on software, computer and technology products bought by parents for home use. However, parents may not be aware that they may be able to reclaim VAT on equipment purchased by them for their children with special needs. In general you can claim VAT relief if:

○ you are an individual with a disability (including dyslexia);

○ the product has been designed solely for people with disabilities;

○ it is for your personal or domestic use.

VAT relief does not apply to products which are designed for ordinary use and happen to be used by someone with a disability. So it does not apply to standard word-processing programs or spreadsheets, but it may apply to the many software products designed for those with special needs. For more details contact HM Revenue and Customs, or see the very useful summary Iansyst provide on their website.

www.iansyst.co.uk/funding/
vatdec/#apply#apply

Chapter 6
Resources

The self-review framework

The British Education Communications and Technology Agency (Becta) is an organisation set up by the government to support strategic ICT development in education. Becta's self-review framework offers schools a structure for improving their effective use of ICT throughout the school. It does this through benchmarking against established best practice and helping to create an action plan for improvement. This self-evaluation is an online tool which assesses the following elements of ICT:

- leadership and management;
- curriculum;
- learning and teaching;
- assessment;
- professional development;
- extending opportunities for learning;
- resources;
- impact on pupil outcomes.

Using this framework can lead to the ICT Mark, an externally assessed quality mark associated with the self-review framework. It recognises a school's reaching a standard of maturity in its use of technology across the school.

Schools working towards the self-review have found it valuable in encouraging the staff and management to work as a team and to develop a coherent development plan. They also recognise its value in integrating with other development within the school. Becta worked with TDA, Ofsted, NCSL, QCA and SSAT to create the framework and ensure common language and goals.

http://schools.becta.org.uk/
index.php?section=srf

You can register and find out more about the framework at the Becta website.

Sources of help
Ability Hub

www.abilityhub.com

This website lists assistive technology designed for people with a disability who find operating a computer difficult or even impossible. The site will also direct you to adaptive equipment and alternative methods for accessing computers.

AbilityNet

www.abilitynet.co.uk

This is a national charity which provides advice on all aspects of computing and disability, including repetitive strain injury (RSI). AbilityNet undertakes assessments as well as running open days for disabled individuals and awareness courses for employers and healthcare professionals. The charity aims to help disabled adults and children use computers and access the Internet by adapting and adjusting their ICT. The website lists products and services on offer and there are fact sheets and articles to download.

www.ace-centre.org.uk

ACE Centre Advisory Trust, Oxford

The Oxford-based ACE Centre Advisory Trust is concerned with the use of technology to meet the communication and educational needs of young people with physical and communication difficulties. Its services include assessments, information, research and development, and specialist training for parents and professionals. The ACE Centre produces a series of guides to software, switches and equipment to support those with communication difficulties.

www.ace-north.org.uk

ACE Centre North

The Oldham-based ACE Centre offers services to enable the effective use of assistive technology for individuals with physical and communication impairments.

www.asbah.org
/2-222-224.aspx

Association for Spina Bifida and Hydrocephalus

ASBAH provides a valuable information sheet for parents and teachers on hydrocephalus and ICT. It covers learning at home and at school and offers some useful software starters.

http://schools.becta.org.uk/
index.php?section=iu
www.capclub.co.uk/games.php

Becta

The Becta website contains advice, guidance and tools to help schools create an inclusive learning environment. The CAP has now closed but the site offers a catalogue of equipment and some helpful online games.

www.bcs.org/server.php?show
=conWebDoc.1252

British Computer Society (BCS) Disability Group

The BCS Disability Group exists to encourage the computer industry to consider the needs of disabled people at the design stage, to identify and correct shortfalls in the provision of equipment, and to stimulate new developments in this field.

www.bdadyslexia.org.uk

British Dyslexia Association

The BDA provides advice for parents, teachers and others supporting children with dyslexia and other language difficulties. They offer some valuable computer information sheets including: Keyboard Awareness and Typing Skills; Supporting Writing with ICT; ICT Starting Points; ICT and Practising Literacy Skills; ICT, Numeracy and Maths; Study Skills; Speech Recognition Software; and Small and Portable Devices.

http://inclusion.ngfl.gov.uk

Inclusion

This site offers advice and sources of help as well as access to 20 online communities which teachers, parents and carers may find helpful.

www.makaton.org/resources/
computer-solutions.htm

Makaton

Makaton offer a range of computer solutions to add signs and symbols to existing computer sets and written text to display as symbols on a computer screen.

www.ncte.ie/SpecialNeedsICT

National Centre for Technology in Education

This website has a section titled 'ICT Training for Special Needs' which contains an abundance of useful information, including details of different types of hardware. The site also has useful links.

www.socsci.ulster.ac.uk/
education/scte/sen/index.html

SCoTENS

The SCoTENS website has a good section on special needs that covers legislation, types of special needs, and ICT and special needs. The ICT section has useful links to products, articles and other SEN websites.

www.senteacher.org/main/
files.php

SEN Teacher Resource

This website for SEN teachers offers free resources for parents and teachers who have children with SEN. These include both printable materials and downloadable software. There are also links to other websites with SEN resources.

www.teem.org.uk

TEEM

This site provides helpful advice on the quality and appropriateness of software. There are up-to-date evaluations of hundreds of educational software packages, all written by practising classroom teachers.

www.widgit.com/SIP/index.htm

Widgit

This site offers a downloadable booklet, 'Warwickshire symbols schools inclusion project', which shows how symbols support inclusion in mainstream education.

www.hitchams.suffolk.sch.uk/
foundation/ict_for_parents.htm

Help for parents

The Sir Robert Hitcham primary school website has a useful ICT guide for parents.

www.capclub.co.uk/games.php
www.gridclub.com/signup/
parents
www.iansyst.co.uk
www.indigolearning.com
www.phonics4parents.co.uk
www.softease.com
www.sherston.co.uk
www.texthelp.com
www.thrass.co.uk
www.widgit.com/parents
www.wordshark.co.uk

Software for home use

Some educational software publishers offer home editions of software, games or activities. The websites listed offer home editions of software or other material that may be of interest to parents.

Suppliers
Relationship with suppliers

Many suppliers are very helpful and will understand your needs. As well as sending the product to you, a specialist supplier is likely to be able to give you advice and help you to make a wise purchase.

When choosing a supplier, it is tempting to focus on the selling price of the product, but there are several other factors you should take into consideration. For example:

❍ If you are purchasing software, it is very helpful to buy from a supplier who offers an evaluation period. This allows you to try out the resource and check it delivers what you require prior to purchase. It also means you can prove its worth to the school budget holder.

❍ If you are buying peripherals or other ICT equipment, consider the after-sales support offered by the supplier, as well as the warranty period. Check that your potential supplier has some sort of email or telephone support service. Website information that offers FAQs (frequently asked questions) can also give an indication of how easy the equipment is to install and use.

The list of suppliers below is not comprehensive, but may provide some useful starting points.

www.2simple.com

2Simple publishes a range of educational software particularly popular with KS1 and SEN children.

www.alphasmart.co.uk

AlphaSmart produces a battery-operated portable word processor with full-size keyboard that links easily to classroom computers.

www.cricksoft.com

Crick Software. The Cricksoft website offers resources to support their products. It includes the Clicker Grids for Learning site.

www.donjohnston.com

Don Johnston supplies a wide range of communication and access devices including BIGmack and Co:Writer. The website has a useful downloads section.

www.granada-learning.com
www.semerc.com

Granada Learning and its associated company SEMERC supply software and hardware for primary, secondary and special education.

www.iansyst.co.uk

iansyst offers independent expert advice on technology to help dyslexic people make the most of their abilities at home and at school, and on into college and the workplace.

www.inclusive.co.uk

Inclusive Technology researches and delivers innovative ICT solutions to the SEN community. It offers specialist consultancy and training as well as supplying a wide range of hardware and software for SEN.

www.independentproducts.co.uk/
special_needs.htm

Independent Products supplies adjustable-height interactive whiteboards, projectors, touch screens and plasma screens.

www.indigolearning.com	**Indigo Learning** produces creative software tools including Dazzle 03 and BuzzWebz, the new website creator.
www.keytools.co.uk	**KeyTools** supplies computer equipment for users with special needs. The range includes specialist keyboards, input devices and mice.
www.r-e-m.co.uk	**REM** is a well-respected distributor of educational software that also supplies resources on behalf of the British Dyslexia Association.
www.sherston.co.uk	**Sherston Software** publishes a wide range of educational software that supports SEN in mainstream schools, including Skill Builders, Leaps and Bounds and LDA Language Cards.
www.taglearning.com	**TAG Learning** produces a special needs catalogue of software and hardware resources, including an educational digital camera and a digital blue video recorder, which are widely used in schools.
www.texthelp.com	**Texthelp** publishes software to assist with reading and writing and to improve literacy skills.
www.tiny-hands.co.uk	**Tiny Hands** provides ergonomic computer peripherals and software designed to minimise the risks associated with increased used of computer equipment among young children.
www.tts-group.co.uk	**TTS Group** supplies ICT resources for Foundation Stage upwards, including Talktime Recordable Postcards.
www.wedgwood-group.com/special_needs.htm	**Wedgwood IT Group** distributes SEN classroom audio-visual equipment, furniture and accessories for schools and colleges.
www.wordshark.co.uk	**White Space** is a software publisher whose products include the well-known Wordshark and Numbershark programs.
www.widgit.com	**Widgit Software** offers special software solutions for communication and, in particular, software that facilitates the creation and use of resources with symbols.

References

Audit Commission (2002) *Special Educational Needs: a mainstream issue*
Becta (2004) *What the Research Says: 2004 ICT provision management and development. ICT and teaching and learning*
DfES (2004) *Every Child Matters: change for children*
DfES (2004) *Removing Barriers to Achievement: the government's strategy for SEN*
DfES (2005) *Harnessing Technology: transforming learning and children's services*